ANNE WILLAN'S
LOOK&COOK
Creative Appetizers

ANNE WILLAN'S
LOOK&COOK

Creative Appetizers

DORLING KINDERSLEY
LONDON • NEW YORK • STUTTGART

A DORLING KINDERSLEY BOOK

Created and Produced by
CARROLL & BROWN LIMITED
5 Lonsdale Road
London NW6 6RA

Editorial Director Jeni Wright
Editors Anna Brandenburger
Stella Vayne
Art Editor Lisa Webb
Designers Lucy De Rosa
Alan Watt
Production Editor Wendy Rogers

First American Edition, 1993
10 9 8 7 6 5 4 3 2 1

Published in the United States by
Dorling Kindersley, Inc., 232 Madison Avenue
New York, New York 10016

Willan, Anne.
    Creative appetizers/ by Anne Willan. – 1st American ed.
    p.   cm. – (Look and cook)
    Includes index.
    ISBN 1-56458-191-8
    1. Cookery (appetizers)   I. Title.   II Series: Willan, Anne.
Look and cook.
TX740.W546 1993
641.8'12 – dc20   92-53452
                                                   CIP

Reproduced by Colourscan, Singapore
Printed and bound in Italy by A. Mondadori, Verona

CONTENTS

APPETIZERS
THE LOOK & COOK APPROACH

Welcome to **Creative Appetizers** and the *Look & Cook* series. These volumes are designed to be the simplest, most informative cookbooks you'll ever own. They are the closest I can come to sharing my personal techniques for cooking my own favorite recipes without actually being with you in the kitchen.

EQUIPMENT

Equipment and ingredients often determine whether or not you can cook a particular dish, so *Look & Cook* sets out everything you need at the beginning of each recipe. You'll see at a glance how long a recipe takes to cook, how many servings it makes, what the finished dish looks like, and how much preparation can be done ahead. When you start to cook, you'll find the preparation and cooking are organized into steps that are easy to follow.

INGREDIENTS

Each stage has its own color coding and everything is shown in photographs with brief text to go with each step. You will never be in doubt as to what it is you are doing, why you are doing it, and how it should look.

🍽 SERVES 4–6   🥣 WORK TIME 25–35 MINUTES   🍲 COOKING TIME 20–30 MINUTES

I've also included helpful hints and ideas under "Anne Says". These may list an alternative ingredient or piece of equipment, or explain a certain method, or add some advice on mastering a particular technique. Similarly, if there is a crucial stage in a recipe when things can go astray, I've included some warnings called "Take Care".

Many of the photographs are annotated to pinpoint why certain pieces of equipment work best, and how food should look at the various stages of cooking. Because presentation is so important, a picture of the finished dish with serving suggestions is at the end of each recipe.

Thanks to all this information, you can't go wrong. I'll be with you every step of the way. So please come with me into the kitchen to look, cook, and enjoy some delicious **Creative Appetizers.**

Anne Willan

WHY APPETIZERS?

First impressions often last longest, so it is important to serve an opening dish that creates the proper mood for what is to come. An appetizer can be as simple as a salad or as special as a soufflé, depending on the occasion and your inclination. The range of recipes is wide. Some appetizers involve a minimum of ingredients and only a few minutes work. Others may take more effort, and require some planning, but you'll find that they all amply repay your attention. For light meals some appetizers can easily become simple main courses.

RECIPE CHOICE

Let the time of year help you decide what appetizer to serve your guests, with warm and hearty first courses to stave off the winter cold, or lighter ideas for a warm summer's day. Review the other dishes in your menu, and choose ingredients that will not be repeated in following courses. Take your cue, too, from cuisines such as French, Asian, Italian, and Mexican, because they will give a lively, offbeat start to any menu. Here are just a few of my own favorites.

COLD FIRST COURSES

Raw Beef Salad with Capers: The Italian classic "carpaccio" features very thinly sliced raw beef served with capers, anchovies, olive oil, and Parmesan cheese curls. *Raw Beef with Basil Sauce:* A "pesto" purée of fresh basil, garlic, pine nuts, Parmesan cheese, and olive oil is served with the very thinly sliced raw beef. *Italian Toasts with Olives, Tomatoes, and Anchovies:* Crostini toasts garnished with fresh basil leaves make a quick and delicious opening to an informal, rustic meal. *Italian Toasts with Arugula and Ricotta:* Peppery arugula, briefly sautéed with sweet balsamic vinegar and combined with creamy ricotta cheese, tops toasted crusty Italian peasant-style bread. *Chinese-Style Stuffed Tomatoes:* The vine-ripened tomatoes of summer have an oriental filling of shrimp, snow peas, and bean sprouts.

Tomatoes Stuffed with Shrimp, Feta, and Black Olives: A colorful first course with a Mediterranean touch. *Stuffed Grape Leaves:* Straight from the Greek Islands, grape leaves are filled with rice, pine nuts, herbs, and raisins. *Lamb-and-Rice-Stuffed Grape Leaves:* Ground lamb replaces the raisins and pine nuts in this meaty version of "dolmades". *Chicken Liver and Apple Pâté:* This luxuriously rich pâté, complemented with diced apples, initiates any meal in an elegant style. *Chicken Liver Pâté with Orange:* Sections of orange are a light topping for an equally rich pâté. *Greek-Style Piquant Vegetables:* Mushrooms and fennel are simmered separately with baby onions, coriander seeds, tomatoes, herbs, and white wine. *Golden Greek-Style Vegetables:* Saffron gives an amber hue to zucchini, cauliflower, and onions. *Smoked Trout Mousse with Horseradish and Dill:* Flakes of smoked trout are the basis for this light mousse, perfect for a buffet luncheon. *Smoked Trout Mousse with Green Peppercorns:* Green peppercorns add a spicier flavor and a touch of color to smoked trout mousse. *Blini with Smoked Salmon:* Traditional Russian treat of small buckwheat pancakes served with a choice of condiments – radishes, capers, onions, and sour cream. *Blini with Red and Black Caviar:* Dazzling tiny beads of caviar in contrasting colors crown more buckwheat pancakes.

WARM FIRST COURSES

Marinated Goat Cheese Salad: A French-style first course of crisp lettuces with rounds of toasted French bread topped with slices of marinated goat cheese. *Breaded Marinated Goat Cheese Salad:* Marinated goat cheese is coated with breadcrumbs, and briefly pan-fried to be served with a salad of watercress and red-leaf lettuce. *Spring Rolls with Lettuce and Mint Leaves:* Crisp packages filled with pork, mushrooms, and cellophane noodles are wrapped in lettuce and fresh mint leaves and served with a hot red pepper dipping sauce – an oriental favorite. *Spring Rolls Filled with Shrimp:* Pink shrimp replaces the pork in these spring rolls served on a bed of grated carrot salad. *Stuffed Mushrooms with Herbs:* Large mushrooms are filled with wild mushrooms, walnuts, garlic, and herbs, then baked until hot and fragrant – a sure winner. *Mushrooms Stuffed with Sun-Dried Tomatoes and Cheese:* A souvenir of sunny Italy, these mushrooms are filled with two cheeses and sun-dried tomatoes and topped with a third cheese. *Cheese Puffs with Spinach and Smoked Salmon:* Cheese choux pastry puffs make delicious containers for a spinach, cream cheese filling, which is then covered with a lattice of smoked salmon. *Cheese Rings Filled with Spinach and Mushrooms:* Rings of choux pastry encase spinach filling accented with sliced mushrooms. *Poached Scallops in Cider Sauce:* Scallops are poached in cider and served in their own shells with a garlic-herb potato border. *Sautéed Scallops with Lemon-Herb Potatoes:* Crisply sautéed scallops partner mashed potatoes with an unusual flavoring of lemon zest. *Herbed Salmon Cakes with Corn Relish:* Flakes of cooked salmon are formed into cakes, then pan-fried to be served with tangy corn relish. *Maryland Crab Cakes:* Take a quick trip to the seashore with this Chesapeake Bay specialty. *Steamed Mussels with Saffron-Cream Sauce:* Cream sauce flavored with saffron threads coats these salty mussels – crusty bread is a must for sopping up the sauce! *Mussels Steamed in White Wine:* Here, the mussels are simply steamed so the cooking liquid makes a delicious broth. *Clams Steamed in White Wine:* As an alternative to mussels, clams are steamed to create a great meal for friends. *Sautéed Onion and Roquefort Tart:* Piquant Roquefort cheese and caramelized onions encased in a

buttery crust will sharpen your appetite. *Cabbage and Goat Cheese Tart:* Fresh goat cheese and shredded cabbage combine in a tasty tart. *Oysters in Champagne Sauce:* A frothy Champagne sauce covers oysters in this elegant presentation. *Oysters Rockefeller:* Spinach stuffing is the hallmark of these baked oysters, claimed to be as rich as the man himself. *Red Cabbage and Bacon Salad with Blue Cheese:* A bistro-style salad of substance with a slight smoky flavor. *Green Cabbage, Walnut, and Bacon Salad:* Chopped walnuts add crunch to finely shredded green cabbage. *Szechuan Sweet and Sour Spareribs:* Pork ribs fried in oil spiced with hot pepper are slowly simmered with oriental flavorings until glazed and tender. *Indonesian Spicy Spareribs:* Ginger and spices give fragrant flavor to the ribs during the same slow cooking. *Mexican Turnovers with Chicken and Cheese:* Tortillas form a handy wrapping for a chicken and cheese filling; fried like quesadillas, they are served with spicy guacamole and tomato-onion garnish. *Mexican Turnovers with Pork:* Pork joins with Cheddar cheese in the filling for these turnovers. *Prosciutto Pizzas with Mozzarella and Basil:* A classic Italian combination of tomato sauce, strips of prosciutto ham, basil leaves, and mozzarella cheese tops these individual pizzas. *Tropical Shrimp Kebabs:* Broiled shrimp on skewers are transformed by a marinade of fresh ginger root, lime juice, and fresh coriander leaves, and served with a spicy peanut sauce. *Vietnamese Shrimp Kebabs:* Balls of puréed shrimp are coated in unsweetend shredded coconut before being baked in the oven and served with peanut sauce. *Cheddar Cheese and Zucchini Soufflé:* Zucchini adds color and Cheddar cheese adds flavor in this special first course. *Onion and Sage Soufflé:* Onions cooked to a purée and flavored with fresh sage are the base for this heartier soufflé.

EQUIPMENT

Appetizer recipes vary widely, and so does the equipment necessary to make them. First priority is a good, sharp chef's knife for chopping. A thin-bladed, flexible slicing knife cuts paper-thin slices of meat and fish, but a long serrated knife or even an electric carving knife can also do the job. In some recipes a food processor will save a considerable amount of time when chopping and puréeing. A blender can usually be used in its place, but the ingredients may need to be worked in batches. Heavy-based saucepans, frying pans, and sauté pans are important. In some oriental recipes a wok will be the cooking utensil of choice. Individual soufflé dishes or ramekins are used as molds or baking dishes in some recipes, other specialized equipment needed for specific recipes includes a terrine mold, a tart pan with removable base, wooden or metal skewers for broiling, and an oyster knife. A few of the recipes call for a pastry bag fitted with a piping tube for shaping mixtures neatly, but instead you can use two spoons or a metal spatula to achieve the same effect .

INGREDIENTS

Vegetables and fruits, meat and seafood, cheese and nuts, there is no end to the amount of ingredients that contribute to creative appetizers. All sorts of vegetables appear, from garden greens, onions, and bell peppers to cabbage and eggplant. Some play a dominant role in recipes such as Stuffed Mushrooms with Herbs. Others form a partnership in dishes like Sautéed Onion and Roquefort Tart, and Red Cabbage and Bacon Salad with Blue Cheese. Delicate shellfish – shrimp, clams, scallops, mussels, and oysters – are luxury favorites, not to mention the smoked salmon and caviar you'll find served with blini . Smoked trout is used to flavor a rich mousse, while fresh salmon is formed into tasty cakes to serve with a tangy corn relish. Recipes featuring poultry and meat in this book include Raw Beef Salad with Capers, Szechuan Sweet and Sour Spareribs, Chicken Liver and Apple Pâté, and Mexican Turnovers with Chicken and Cheese. Lively, salty, and tart seasonings are often key ingredients in appetizers. Cheeses such as Roquefort, goat, Parmesan, and Cheddar give a rich flavor to several dishes including Marinated Goat Cheese Salad. A piquant accent is added to many recipes with capers, garlic, fresh hot chili peppers, and even fresh horseradish. Vinegar and fresh lemon juice

enliven other recipes, such as Greek-Style Piquant Vegetables and Stuffed Grape Leaves. The more prized ingredients are caviar, saffron, and Champagne; they are used in small quantities to add an opening touch of elegance for a grand occasion.

TECHNIQUES

The techniques used in this book are as varied as the recipes. You'll be doing a good deal of chopping, slicing, and shaping ingredients for attractive presentations. Some dishes require only a little cooking, relying simply on blanching, toasting, or quick sautéing. Shellfish are rapidly cooked by poaching, broiling, and steaming. Marinating in wine or lemon juice, oil, and a variety of seasonings is a practical technique that adds flavor and tenderness before cooking. Just occasionally, as in Raw Beef Salad with Capers, the ingredients may be served without any cooking at all. Stove-top preparations include the blanching and simmering of vegetables, and pan-frying of food such as salmon cakes and Mexican Turnovers with Chicken and Cheese. The oven comes into play for cooking soufflés and when baking pastry tarts, choux puffs, and toasts for crostini. You will also learn how to make an assortment of sauces and accompaniments, including guacamole, Indonesian peanut sauce, vinaigrette dressing, corn relish, and flavored mashed potatoes. As with other volumes in the *Look & Cook* series, we describe in detail the basic techniques that are commonly used in these recipes. You will see how to chop herbs; how to peel, seed, and chop tomatoes; how to chop onions and shallots; how to core, seed, and dice bell peppers and fresh hot chili peppers; how to chop ginger and garlic; and how to core, peel, and dice apples. Decorative ideas include how to make a scallion brush.

RAW BEEF SALAD WITH CAPERS

Carpaccio Piccante

🍴 SERVES 4   🥄 WORK TIME 20–25 MINUTES*

EQUIPMENT

slicing knife

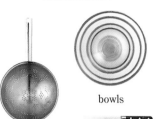
aluminum foil†

colander

bowls

chef's knife

paper towels

vegetable peeler

strainer

pepper mill

citrus
juicer

chopping board

---

†wax paper or plastic wrap can
also be used

ANNE SAYS
*"Instead of the slicing knife,
I find an electric knife is also
excellent for slicing the beef
paper-thin."*

For Italian-style "carpaccio", lean beef tenderloin
is semi-frozen so it is easy to cut into paper-thin
slices – so thin, it's said, that light will show
through. Garnishes here include capers,
anchovies, chopped onion, and fruity extra-virgin
olive oil, with shavings of Parmesan cheese.
Success depends on the freshest lean beef.

GETTING AHEAD

The beef can be sliced and arranged on plates up to
1 hour ahead, provided it is kept, tightly covered,
in the refrigerator.

*plus 2½–3 hours freezing time

SHOPPING LIST

1 lb	piece of beef tenderloin
8	canned anchovy fillets
¼ cup	drained capers
1	small onion
4 oz	piece of Parmesan cheese
4 oz	arugula
2	lemons
½ cup	extra-virgin olive oil, more to taste
	freshly ground black pepper for serving

INGREDIENTS

beef tenderloin

capers

arugula†

olive oil

large piece of
Parmesan
cheese

anchovy
fillets

black peppercorns

lemons

onion

†curly endive or any tart salad
greens can also be used

ANNE SAYS
*"By starting with a large
piece of Parmesan cheese
you'll find it easier to make
the curls. Keep what is left
for grating."*

ORDER OF WORK

1 FREEZE THE BEEF
AND PREPARE
THE GARNISH
INGREDIENTS

2 ASSEMBLE THE
CARPACCIO

1 FREEZE THE BEEF AND PREPARE THE GARNISH INGREDIENTS

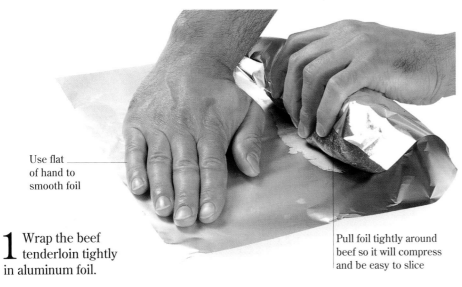

Use flat of hand to smooth foil

1 Wrap the beef tenderloin tightly in aluminum foil.

Pull foil tightly around beef so it will compress and be easy to slice

2 Twist the ends of the foil to seal well, then freeze until firm but not frozen solid, 2½–3 hours.

3 Meanwhile, drain the anchovies and spread out on paper towels. If the capers are large, coarsely chop them. Peel the onion, and cut it in half with the chef's knife. Slice each half horizontally, then vertically; cut across the onion to make dice. Continue chopping until very fine.

4 Using the vegetable peeler, shave 12 large strips from the piece of Parmesan cheese.

5 Wash the arugula in plenty of cold water. Discard any tough stems, and drain the leaves well in the colander. Wrap the arugula in paper towels or a dish towel and keep in the refrigerator.

Arugula leaves will not wilt if wrapped loosely in paper towels and kept in refrigerator

2 ASSEMBLE THE CARPACCIO

1 Arrange the arugula in a single layer around the edge of 4 individual plates, leaving the center of each plate open.

Arugula leaves make pretty display

2 Take the beef from the freezer and unwrap it. If the meat is too hard to cut, let it thaw slightly at room temperature.

3 Using the slicing knife, cut paper-thin slices from the tenderloin. Slice as much of the meat as you can; there will be a little left at the end.

ANNE SAYS
"Use the remaining meat for another recipe, or chop it finely to make steak tartare to serve with the carpaccio."

Paper-thin tenderloin slices allow light to shine through

4 As you slice the beef, arrange it, slightly overlapping in the center of the plates. Curl the anchovy fillets into rings and put 2 in the center of each plate.

! TAKE CARE !
The beef is very delicate when sliced; it should be transferred to the plates directly after slicing.

5 On each serving, fill 1 anchovy ring with chopped onion and the other with capers.

Mound capers carefully so anchovy rings keep their shape

6 Squeeze the juice from the lemons; there should be 6 tbsp juice. Spoon the lemon juice over the beef.

7 Sprinkle the olive oil over the beef. Arrange the Parmesan cheese curls on top.

Raw beef glistens with olive oil

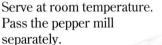 **TO SERVE**
Serve at room temperature. Pass the pepper mill separately.

Capers and onion, enclosed in rings of anchovy, add piquancy to salad

Crisp green arugula makes perfect background for beef

VARIATION

RAW BEEF WITH BASIL SAUCE

Pesto is a treasured sauce, concentrated in flavor and useful in a wide variety of dishes.

1 Wrap and freeze the beef as directed in the main recipe.
2 Meanwhile, make the pesto sauce: strip the leaves from 1 large bunch of fresh basil (about 3 oz), reserving 4 sprigs for garnish. Put the basil in a food processor with 4 peeled garlic cloves, $1/2$ cup grated Parmesan cheese, $1/4$ cup pine nuts, 1 tsp salt, and pepper. Purée until smooth. With the blades turning, gradually add $3/4$ cup olive oil. Taste for seasoning.
3 Make the Parmesan cheese shavings as directed.
4 Thinly slice the beef and arrange it, overlapping, on each plate, omitting the arugula.
5 Squeeze the juice of 1 lemon over the beef and spoon a little pesto in the center of each plate.
6 Arrange the Parmesan shavings on top and decorate with the reserved basil sprigs. Serve the remaining pesto separately.

ITALIAN TOASTS WITH OLIVES, TOMATOES, AND ANCHOVIES

Crostini alla Siciliana

🍴 SERVES 8 🥣 WORK TIME 15–20 MINUTES* 🍲 BAKING TIME 5–10 MINUTES

EQUIPMENT

olive pitter

bread knife

slotted spoon

large metal spoon

chef's knife

saucepan

small knife

bowls

baking sheet

chopping board

plastic wrap

Crostini are an Italian inspiration with an unlimited variety of toppings. Here chopped tomatoes are marinated with olive oil, basil, and garlic, then mixed with olives and anchovies. Authentic crostini call for Italian peasant-style bread, but you can substitute any crusty loaf that has a chewy center.

plus 30–60 minutes standing time

INGREDIENTS

peasant-style bread

black olives

tomatoes

fresh basil

olive oil

anchovy fillets

garlic cloves

ANNE SAYS
"The choice of olive oil depends on the style of cooking. The more assertive fragrance of the better quality unrefined oils is best in these crostini."

SHOPPING LIST

1¹/₂ lb	ripe tomatoes
1	small bunch of fresh basil
4	garlic cloves
	salt and pepper
¹/₄ cup	extra-virgin olive oil
4	canned anchovy fillets
1 cup	Italian or Greek-style black olives
1	small loaf of Italian peasant-style bread

ORDER OF WORK

1 **PREPARE THE TOPPING**

2 **MAKE THE CROSTINI**

---

1 PREPARE THE TOPPING

1 Cut the cores from the tomatoes and score an "x" on the base of each with the tip of the small knife. Immerse in a pan of boiling water until the skin starts to split, 8–15 seconds, depending on their ripeness. Using the slotted spoon, transfer them at once to a bowl of cold water. When cold, peel off the skin. Cut the tomatoes crosswise in half, squeeze out the seeds, then coarsely chop.

2 Strip the basil leaves from the stems, reserving 8 sprigs for garnish, and pile them on the chopping board. Coarsely chop the leaves. Peel and finely chop the garlic (see box, below).

Be careful not to bruise tender basil leaves

HOW TO PEEL AND CHOP GARLIC

The strength of garlic varies with its age and dryness; use more when it is very fresh.

1 Separate the cloves from the bulb by pulling with your fingers. Alternatively, separate the cloves by crushing the bulb with the heel of your hand.

Garlic cloves are easily separated

2 Lightly crush the clove with a chef's knife to loosen the skin.

3 Carefully peel the loosened skin from the clove with your fingers, and discard. Set the flat side of the knife on top of the clove and strike firmly with your fist.

4 Finely chop the garlic with the chef's knife, moving the knife blade back and forth.

3 Combine the chopped tomatoes, garlic, and basil in a bowl. Add a little salt and pepper with the olive oil.

For best flavor use extra-virgin olive oil

Chopped tomatoes, garlic, and basil are coated with golden olive oil

Special tool makes olive pitting easy

6 Pit the olives and coarsely chop them with the chef's knife.

4 Stir to mix the ingredients together, then cover and let stand at room temperature, 30–60 minutes.

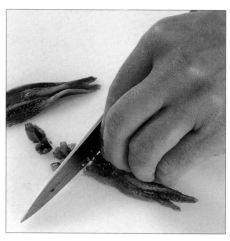

5 Meanwhile, gather the anchovy fillets together with your fingers and chop them crosswise.

ANNE SAYS
"If you like, you can chop the anchovies in a food processor, and the olives too, but be careful not to overwork them or they will become a purée."

7 Stir the olives and anchovies into the tomatoes. Taste for seasoning and adjust if necessary.

2 MAKE THE CROSTINI

1 Heat the oven to 400° F. Cut the bread into eight ½-inch-thick slices. Spread out the slices on the baking sheet and toast until lightly browned, turning once, 5–10 minutes.

Cut generous slices so bread does not dry out too much in oven

2 Spoon the tomato, olive and anchovy topping on the toasted bread, spreading it roughly. Garnish each crostini with a basil sprig.

🍴 TO SERVE

Arrange the crostini on a platter and serve warm or at room temperature.

Basil leaves add fresh green garnish

ITALIAN TOASTS WITH ARUGULA AND RICOTTA

1 Omit the tomatoes, basil, olives, and anchovies.

2 Wash ¾ lb arugula and discard any tough stems. Tear the leaves into large pieces. Chop 3 garlic cloves.

3 Heat 2 tbsp olive oil in a frying pan, add the arugula, garlic, salt, and pepper, and cook, stirring constantly, just until arugula has wilted, about 2–3 minutes. Add 3–4 tbsp balsamic vinegar and simmer 1 minute.

4 Drain the arugula in a colander and coarsely chop the leaves. Transfer them to a bowl and stir in ¾ cup ricotta cheese. Season to taste.

5 Slice and toast the peasant-style bread as directed in the main recipe. Spread the arugula mixture on top, cut each slice in half, and serve warm, decorated with tomato wedges and black olives if you like.

Warm toasted bread is crunchy base for crostini topping

GETTING AHEAD

The topping can be prepared up to 3–4 hours ahead and kept, covered, at room temperature. Assemble the crostini just before serving so the toasted bread does not get soggy.

CHINESE-STYLE STUFFED TOMATOES

🍽 SERVES 6 ⌛ WORK TIME 30–35 MINUTES*

EQUIPMENT

bowls

chef's knife

whisk

medium
saucepan

small knife

large metal spoon

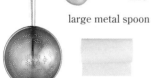

colander

paper towels

chopping board

An ideal first course for the vine-ripened tomatoes of summer. The tomatoes are filled with shrimp and bean sprouts tossed in a soy and ginger vinaigrette, then arranged with a "fan" of snow peas for a brilliant, colorful effect.

GETTING AHEAD

The vinaigrette can be made up to 1 week ahead.
The remaining ingredients can be prepared 1 day ahead
and refrigerated. Assemble the salads not more than
1 hour before serving.

*plus 30 minutes standing time

INGREDIENTS

peeled cooked shrimp

tomatoes   fresh ginger root

sesame oil

vegetable oil

bean sprouts

white wine
vinegar†

snow peas   garlic

soy sauce

scallions

†cider vinegar can also be used

SHOPPING LIST

6	medium tomatoes, total weight about 2¼ lb
6 oz	snow peas
¼ lb	bean sprouts, about 1½ cups
3	scallions
½ lb	peeled cooked shrimp
	salt and pepper
	For the vinaigrette
½-inch	piece of fresh ginger root
1	garlic clove
2 tbsp	white wine vinegar
2 tsp	soy sauce
1 tsp	sesame oil
⅓ cup	vegetable oil

ORDER OF WORK

1 PREPARE THE
TOMATOES AND
VINAIGRETTE

2 PREPARE THE
STUFFING AND
STUFF THE
TOMATOES

1 PREPARE THE TOMATOES AND VINAIGRETTE

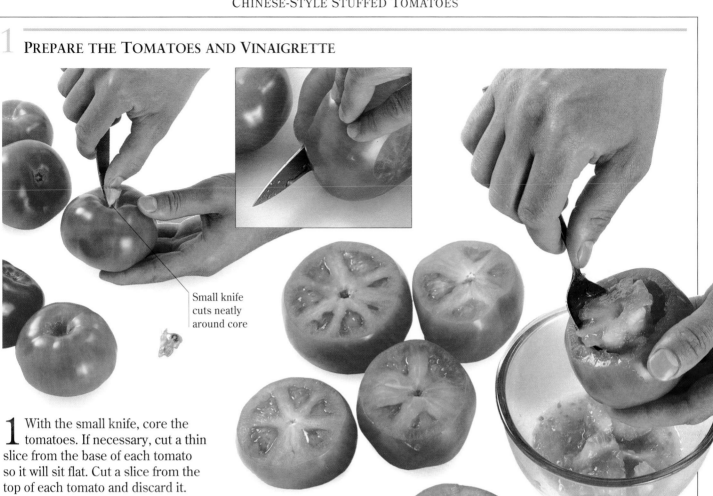

Small knife cuts neatly around core

Ripe but firm tomatoes make good cups for stuffing

1 With the small knife, core the tomatoes. If necessary, cut a thin slice from the base of each tomato so it will sit flat. Cut a slice from the top of each tomato and discard it.

2 Scrape out and discard the tomato seeds and flesh with a tablespoon, leaving a ¼-inch shell. Sprinkle the inside of the tomatoes with salt. Set the tomatoes upside down on paper towels. Let stand 30 minutes. Meanwhile, make the vinaigrette and prepare the stuffing.

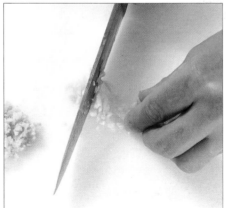

3 Make the vinaigrette: peel the ginger. With the chef's knife, slice the ginger, cutting across the fibrous grain. Crush each slice with the flat of the knife and finely chop.

4 Lightly crush the garlic clove to loosen the skin. Peel off the skin with your fingertips and discard. Finely chop the garlic using the chef's knife.

5 In a small bowl, whisk together the ginger, garlic, vinegar, soy sauce, and sesame oil. Gradually whisk in the vegetable oil so the vinaigrette emulsifies and thickens slightly. Season the dressing with salt and pepper, and set aside.

2 PREPARE THE STUFFING AND STUFF THE TOMATOES

1 With your fingers, trim the stem end from each of the snow peas and pull the string down the pod. Trim the other end. Discard the trimmings.

2 Half fill the saucepan with cold salted water and bring to a boil. Add the snow peas and simmer until just tender, 3–4 minutes. Drain, rinse with cold water, and drain again.

3 Reserve two-thirds of the snow peas in a bowl. Stack the remaining snow peas and cut across into ¼-inch slices with the chef's knife.

4 Pick over the bean sprouts and put them in a bowl. Pour boiling water over the sprouts and let stand 2 minutes. Drain, rinse with cold water, and drain again thoroughly. Coarsely chop the bean sprouts.

5 Trim the roots and coarse green tops from the scallions. Remove any outer skin and discard, then coarsely chop them.

6 Coarsely chop the shrimp, reserving 3 large whole shrimp for garnish. Cut the reserved whole shrimp lengthwise in half.

Whole shrimp make sumptuous garnish

Chop shrimp coarsely so stuffing has texture

7 Combine the chopped snow peas, bean sprouts, scallions, shrimp, and vinaigrette and toss to mix. Taste for seasoning. Lightly season the inside of the tomatoes, then fill with stuffing.

Divide stuffing equally among tomatoes

 TO SERVE

Arrange the reserved snow peas in a fan on each of 6 individual plates. Put a filled tomato on each plate, and garnish with a halved shrimp. If you like, decorate each serving with a scallion brush (see box, page 99).

Fan of lush green snow peas forms base for delicious stuffed tomato

TOMATOES STUFFED WITH SHRIMP, FETA, AND BLACK OLIVES

1 Prepare the tomatoes as directed in the main recipe.
2 Make the vinaigrette: whisk together 2 tbsp red wine vinegar, 1–2 tsp Dijon-style mustard, salt, and pepper. Gradually whisk in ⅓ cup olive oil so the dressing emulsifies and thickens slightly.
3 Omit the snow peas and bean sprouts. Bring a pan of cold salted water to a boil, add ½ cup rice, and bring back to a boil. Simmer until just tender, stirring occasionally, 10–12 minutes. Drain the rice, rinse with cold water, and drain again thoroughly. Let the rice cool 8–10 minutes, then fluff with a fork and let chill in the refrigerator.
4 Coarsely chop 5–6 pitted black olives. Strip the leaves from 10–12 sprigs of fresh coriander (cilantro) and pile them on a chopping board. With a chef's knife, coarsely chop the leaves. Crumble 1½ oz feta cheese into a bowl. Chop the scallions and coarsely chop all of the shrimp.
5 Add the chopped black olives and coriander to the feta, with the scallions, shrimp, rice, and vinaigrette; toss to mix. Add 1–2 tsp anise-flavored liqueur, if you like, and season to taste with salt and pepper.
6 Fill the prepared tomatoes with the stuffing, using a spoon.
7 Serve each tomato on a curly salad leaf. Decorate the plate with tender Belgian endive leaves and fresh herbs, if you like.

STUFFED GRAPE LEAVES

Dolmades

SERVES 8   **WORK TIME 40–45 MINUTES***   **COOKING TIME 45–60 MINUTES**

EQUIPMENT

colander

large sauté pan with lid†

strainer

large metal spoon

citrus juicer

chef's knife

heatproof plate

wooden spoon

small knife

paper towels

non-metallic dish

bowls

baking sheet

saucepans

metal skewer

†deep frying pan or skillet can also be used

Grape leaves, stuffed with seasoned rice, are one of the great first courses found around the Mediterranean, especially in Greece. Fresh leaves can be found in the summer months; they must be steamed or blanched before use. Grape leaves are also available year-round canned, vacuum-packed, and bottled in brine. This classic filling includes pine nuts, golden raisins, fresh dill, and mint.

GETTING AHEAD
The stuffed leaves can be cooked up to 3 days ahead and kept in the refrigerator.

plus 12 hours marinating time

INGREDIENTS

grape leaves

chicken stock   onions

lemons

fresh mint

long-grain rice

pine nuts

olive oil

fresh dill

golden raisins

SHOPPING LIST

40	grape leaves packed in brine, more if needed
3 cups	chicken stock or water, more if needed
	For the stuffing
¹/₂ cup	pine nuts
	salt and pepper
1 cup	long-grain rice
2	medium onions
1	medium bunch of fresh dill
1	small bunch of fresh mint
2	lemons
³/₄ cup	olive oil
¹/₃ cup	golden raisins

ORDER OF WORK

1 MAKE THE STUFFING

2 STUFF THE GRAPE LEAVES

3 COOK AND FINISH THE STUFFED GRAPE LEAVES

1 MAKE THE STUFFING

Toasting pine nuts enhances their flavor

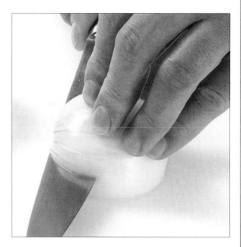

1 Heat the oven to 375°F. Toast the pine nuts on the baking sheet until lightly browned, stirring occasionally so they color evenly, 5–8 minutes.

! TAKE CARE !
Do not let the pine nuts burn or they will be bitter.

2 Bring a medium saucepan of salted water to a boil. Add the rice and bring back to a boil. Simmer until the rice is just tender, 10–12 minutes. Stir occasionally to prevent the rice from sticking to the bottom of the pan.

3 Meanwhile, peel the onions, leaving a little of the root attached, and cut them in half through root and stem. Lay each onion half flat on the chopping board and slice horizontally toward the root, leaving the slices attached at the root end.

4 Slice vertically, again leaving the root end intact. Then cut across the onion to make dice, guiding the knife with your knuckles.

Dill and mint are classic flavoring herbs for stuffed grape leaves

5 Strip the herb leaves from the stems, reserving a few small dill and mint sprigs for garnish, and pile them on the chopping board. With the chef's knife, coarsely chop the leaves. Squeeze the juice from the lemons; there should be 6 tbsp juice.

6 Drain the rice in the strainer, rinse with cold water to wash away the starch, and drain again thoroughly.

7 Heat one-third of the oil in a large saucepan. Add the onions and cook, until soft but not brown, 3–5 minutes.

Stir rice stuffing well to mix ingredients before tasting for seasoning

Golden raisins add hint of sweetness to stuffing

8 Stir in the rice, toasted pine nuts, golden raisins, chopped herbs, one-quarter of the lemon juice, salt, and pepper. Taste for seasoning.

ANNE SAYS

"*Be sure that the stuffing mixture is highly seasoned at this stage because the flavors will mellow and become subdued during cooking.*"

2 STUFF THE GRAPE LEAVES

1 Bring a saucepan of water to a boil. Put the grape leaves in a bowl and cover with boiling water.

2 Separate the leaves with the wooden spoon. Let the leaves stand in the water 15 minutes or according to package directions.

3 Drain the leaves in the colander, rinse with cold water, and drain again thoroughly.

4 Place the grape leaves in layers between sheets of paper towels and pat gently to dry.

Blanched grape leaves are supple and will be easy to roll

Paper towels absorb excess water from grape leaves

! TAKE CARE !
The grape leaves can be torn easily, so handle them gently.

5 Spread about 8 grape leaves over the bottom of the sauté pan to prevent the stuffed leaves from sticking to the pan.

Rice stuffing is full of golden raisins and nuts

6 Spread 1 of the remaining grape leaves flat on the work surface, vein-side up with the stem end toward you. Put 1–2 spoonfuls rice stuffing in the center of the leaf.

7 Fold the sides and stem end of the leaf over the stuffing. Starting at the stem end, roll up the leaf away from you into a neat cylinder enclosing all the stuffing. Repeat with the remaining leaves and stuffing.

ANNE SAYS
"If the leaves are small, use 2 leaves for each roll and slightly overlap them."

Grape leaves roll into neat packages

3 COOK AND FINISH THE STUFFED GRAPE LEAVES

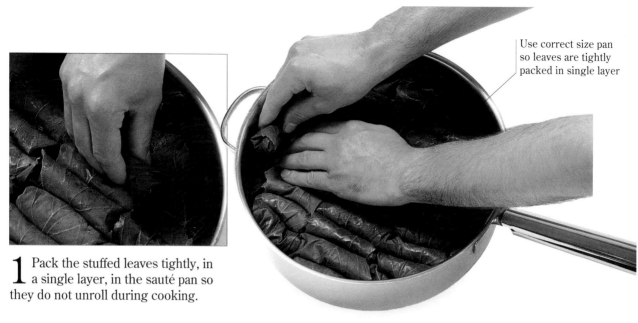

Use correct size pan so leaves are tightly packed in single layer

1 Pack the stuffed leaves tightly, in a single layer, in the sauté pan so they do not unroll during cooking.

Chicken stock imparts extra flavor to rolls

2 Pour the chicken stock or water over the grape leaves. Add half of the remaining oil and half of the remaining lemon juice.

ANNE SAYS
"The liquid prevents the leaves from drying out and ensures even cooking."

Pour in stock to just cover leaves

Leaves are covered with liquid throughout cooking

3 Cover the grape leaves with the heatproof plate. Bring to a boil on top of the stove, then cover the pan with the lid, and simmer over low heat, 45–60 minutes.

! TAKE CARE !
The stuffed leaves must always be covered with liquid so you may need to add more water during cooking.

4 To test when done, pierce the leaves with the skewer; they should be very tender. Let stuffed grape leaves cool in the saucepan.

5 Transfer the cooked leaves to the non-metallic dish. Spoon over any remaining cooking liquid, cover, and marinate in the refrigerator at least 12 hours so the flavors can mellow.

Cooking liquid keeps stuffed grape leaves moist while they marinate

🍴 **TO SERVE**

Set the stuffed grape leaves on a serving platter and spoon over the remaining olive oil and lemon juice. Garnish with the reserved dill and mint sprigs, plus rings of red, yellow, and green bell pepper, if you like.

Lemon juice and fruity olive oil give shine to stuffed grape leaves

Grape leaves enclose tasty stuffing of rice, pine nuts, raisins, and herbs

V A R I A T I O N

LAMB-AND-RICE-STUFFED GRAPE LEAVES

Ground lamb and spices add substance to the filling for grape leaves here, which are served with a simple yogurt and chopped mint sauce.

1 Omit the pine nuts, fresh dill, and golden raisins from the stuffing.
2 Cook ¾ cup rice as directed.
3 Meanwhile, sauté the chopped onions in ¼ cup olive oil. Add ¾ lb ground lamb to the softened onions and cook, stirring, until it loses its pink color, 5–7 minutes.
4 Chop the leaves from a large bunch of fresh mint.

5 Add the rice, chopped mint, juice of ½ lemon, ½ tsp ground cinnamon, a pinch of ground nutmeg, salt, and pepper to the lamb mixture; stir to mix.
6 Stuff the grape leaves as directed, using small leaves or cutting larger leaves lengthwise in half. Cook as directed, using water instead of stock.
7 Serve warm, with a plain yogurt and chopped mint sauce. Garnish with fresh mint, if you like.

CHICKEN LIVER AND APPLE PATE

 SERVES 6　 WORK TIME 30–35 MINUTES*　COOKING TIME 12–15 MINUTES

EQUIPMENT

 ½-cup
ramekins

food
processor†

apple corer

vegetable peeler

frying pan

bowls

small knife

chef's knife

metal spatula

3-inch
cookie
cutter

2-pronged
fork

rubber spatula

chopping board

wooden spoon

metal spoon

slotted spoon

†blender can also be used

The smooth richness of the chicken livers is pleasantly contrasted with the sweet sautéed apples. A touch of Calvados or Cognac is added and then flamed for depth of flavor. Topped with a golden slice of caramelized apple, these individual pâtés make an elegant first course.

GETTING AHEAD

The chicken liver pâté can be kept up to 2 days, covered, in the refrigerator, and the flavor will mellow. Prepare the decoration and add just before serving.

*plus 2–3 hours chilling time

SHOPPING LIST

4	shallots
2	garlic cloves
1 lb	chicken livers
3	medium dessert apples
1 cup	butter
	salt and pepper
¼ cup	Calvados
2 tbsp	sugar
6	sprigs of fresh mint for decoration
6	slices of whole-wheat bread

INGREDIENTS

chicken
livers

shallots

Calvados†

garlic

dessert apples

butter

whole-wheat
bread

sugar

mint

†Cognac can also be used

ORDER OF WORK

1 PREPARE THE
INGREDIENTS

2 MAKE THE
CHICKEN LIVER
PATE

3 PREPARE THE
GARNISH

1 PREPARE THE INGREDIENTS

Cook apples briskly so they keep their shape

1 Peel the shallots, set flat-side down and slice. Then chop them to make fine dice. Discard the skin from the garlic cloves and finely chop the garlic.

2 Trim any membrane from the chicken livers with the small knife. Core, peel, and dice 2 of the apples (see box, below).

3 Melt 2 tbsp butter in the frying pan. Add the diced apples, salt, and pepper to the pan.

HOW TO CORE, PEEL, AND DICE APPLES

If you remove an apple core using a corer, the fruit is left whole and easy to dice.

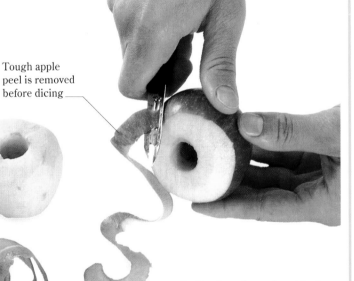

Tough apple peel is removed before dicing

1 Force the apple corer sharply down through each apple to cut out the core.

2 Peel each apple with the vegetable peeler, then cut into ³⁄₈-inch slices.

3 Stack the slices of apple, 2 or 3 at a time, on a chopping board and using a chef's knife cut across into medium strips.

4 Gather the strips of apple together in a pile with your fingertips, and cut across to produce medium dice.

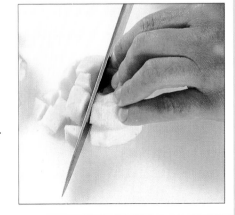

Diced apples add hint of sweetness to chicken liver pâté

4 Sauté the apples, stirring frequently, until tender, 5–7 minutes. Transfer the diced apples to a bowl with the slotted spoon.

Apples cook in butter until slightly soft and golden

5 Melt another 2 tbsp butter in the frying pan. Add the chicken livers, salt, and pepper to the pan. Fry the livers, stirring, over medium heat until brown on the outside, 2–3 minutes.

6 Scrape the chopped garlic and shallots into the frying pan.

7 Continue cooking the livers, garlic, and shallots, stirring, until the shallots are slightly softened, 1–2 minutes.

Fry livers rapidly so they remain pink in center

8 Remove a liver from the frying pan, then slice into it to test whether it is cooked. It should be very brown on the outside, but still pink in the center.

9 Increase the heat to medium-high. Pour the Calvados into the pan and bring to a boil.

Crisp particles in bottom of pan are loosened by adding Calvados

10 Hold a lighted match to the pan's side to flame the alcohol alight.

! TAKE CARE !
Flames can rise quite high, so stand back from the pan. Use a long-handled spoon for basting.

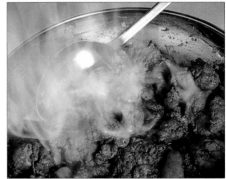

11 Baste the chicken livers until the flames subside, 20–30 seconds. Let the livers cool.

2 MAKE THE CHICKEN LIVER PATE

1 Purée the chicken liver mixture in the food processor until almost smooth. Wipe the pan clean.

ANNE SAYS
"Little bits of crispy liver from the pan add texture to the pâté."

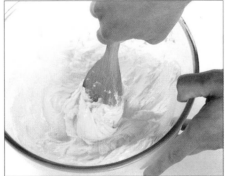

2 With the wooden spoon or an electric mixer, cream 10 tbsp butter until very soft.

3 Add the chicken liver purée, with the diced and sautéed apples, to the creamed butter in the bowl.

4 Using the wooden spoon, mix the ingredients together thoroughly. Season the pâté to taste.

5 Spoon the pâté into six ramekins, filling them at least three-quarters full. Smooth the tops with the back of a spoon dipped in hot water so it does not stick to the pâté. Cover and chill until firm, 2–3 hours. Meanwhile, prepare the garnish.

Back of spoon dipped in hot water makes surface of pâté smooth

3 PREPARE THE GARNISH

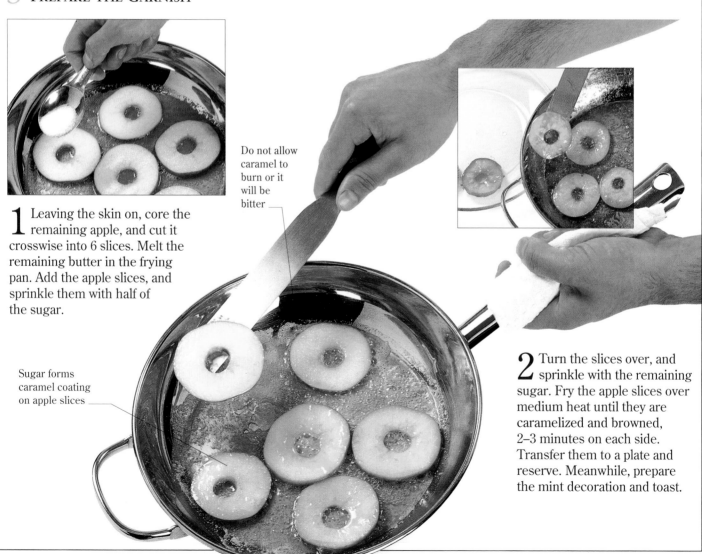

1 Leaving the skin on, core the remaining apple, and cut it crosswise into 6 slices. Melt the remaining butter in the frying pan. Add the apple slices, and sprinkle them with half of the sugar.

Do not allow caramel to burn or it will be bitter

Sugar forms caramel coating on apple slices

2 Turn the slices over, and sprinkle with the remaining sugar. Fry the apple slices over medium heat until they are caramelized and browned, 2–3 minutes on each side. Transfer them to a plate and reserve. Meanwhile, prepare the mint decoration and toast.

Mint sprigs bring fresh aroma and color to finished dish

3 Holding the mint stems in one hand, remove the top sprigs of leaves with your fingers.

4 Toast the slices of whole-wheat bread. Cut out large circles from the toast using the cookie cutter, or cut the slices into triangles if you prefer.

¶⊙¶ TO SERVE
Set a caramelized apple slice and a mint sprig on top of each pâté and serve with the toast.

Caramelized apple echoes flavoring in pâté

Whole-wheat toast is a classic accompaniment to chicken liver pâté

VARIATION
CHICKEN LIVER PATE WITH ORANGE
Ramekins, small cups, molds, or pots, 2-inches deep, make ideal containers for this plain chicken liver pâté, topped with orange sections.

1 Omit the apples and sugar. Make the pâté as directed, using only 3/4 cup butter and using Cointreau or Grand Marnier instead of the Calvados. Spoon the pâté into the chosen containers, then chill them.

2 Section 1 orange for decoration: slice off the top and bottom of the orange. Cut away the peel and white pith, following the curve of the fruit. Working over a bowl, cut down each side of the orange sections to separate them from the membranes, discarding the seeds as you go. Put the sections on a plate, cover, and refrigerate.

3 Just before serving, top each of the ramekins with 2 orange sections, and accompany with triangles of toasted whole-wheat bread.

GREEK-STYLE PIQUANT VEGETABLES

Légumes à la grecque

🍽 SERVES 6–8 🥣 WORK TIME 25–30 MINUTES 🍲 COOKING TIME 25–30 MINUTES

EQUIPMENT

bowls

kitchen string

cheesecloth

2 sauté pans†

whisk

colander

large metal spoon

chef's knife

saucepan

small knife   wooden stirrer

paper towels

chopping board

†deep frying pans can also be used

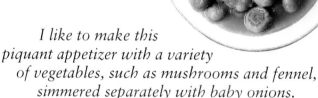

I like to make this piquant appetizer with a variety of vegetables, such as mushrooms and fennel, simmered separately with baby onions.

— GETTING AHEAD —

The vegetables can be cooked up to 2 days ahead and kept in the refrigerator. The flavors mellow on standing.

SHOPPING LIST

1 lb	tomatoes
24	baby onions
1 lb	button mushrooms
1 lb	fennel bulbs
¼ cup	vegetable oil
¼ cup	olive oil
	salt and pepper
⅓ cup	raisins
	For the spice bags and cooking liquid
¼ cup	coriander seeds
1 tbsp	black peppercorns
4	bay leaves
5–7	sprigs of fresh thyme
3–4	sprigs of parsley
2 tbsp	tomato paste
3 cups	chicken stock or water, more if needed
	juice of 1 lemon
¼ cup	dry white wine

INGREDIENTS

button mushrooms   tomatoes

baby onions   raisins

fennel bulbs

vegetable oil   olive oil

bay leaves   dry white wine   black peppercorns

tomato paste

parsley

coriander seeds   chicken stock

lemon juice

fresh thyme

ORDER OF WORK

1 PREPARE THE INGREDIENTS

2 COOK THE ONIONS AND MUSHROOMS

3 COOK THE ONIONS AND FENNEL

1 PREPARE THE INGREDIENTS

Flavorings tied in cheesecloth will be easy to remove when cooking is finished

1 Combine the coriander seeds, black peppercorns, bay leaves, thyme sprigs, and parsley sprigs. Halve the mixture and tie each portion up in a piece of cheesecloth.

2 Make the cooking liquid: whisk the tomato paste, half of the chicken stock or water, the lemon juice, and white wine in a bowl.

3 Core the tomatoes. Score an "x" on the base of each. Immerse in boiling water, 8–15 seconds. Transfer to cold water, reserving the hot water. When cooled, peel and cut crosswise in half. Squeeze out the seeds, then coarsely chop each half.

4 Put the baby onions in a bowl, cover with the hot water, and let stand 2 minutes. Drain and peel them, leaving a little of the root attached.

6 Wash each fennel bulb; trim the stems and roots, discarding any tough outer pieces from the bulbs. Cut the fennel bulbs lengthwise in half. Set each half cut-side down and slice.

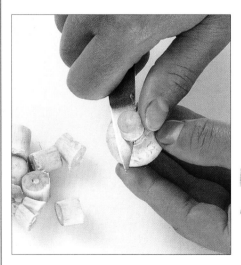

5 Wipe the mushroom caps with damp paper towels and trim the stems level with the caps. Cut the caps into quarters if large.

Fennel adds subtle licorice flavor

2 COOK THE ONIONS AND MUSHROOMS

1 Heat half of the vegetable oil and half of the olive oil in a sauté pan. Add half of the baby onions and sauté until lightly browned, about 3 minutes.

Tomatoes will reduce down, adding color and flavor to sauce

2 Add the mushrooms, a spice bag, and the chopped tomatoes to the sauté pan.

3 Pour in half of the cooking liquid – there should be enough to almost cover the vegetables; if necessary, add more stock or water. Add salt. Bring to a fast boil over high heat.

Use tip of knife to test vegetables for tenderness

4 Continue boiling rapidly, stirring occasionally. Add a little stock or water as the liquid evaporates, so the vegetables do not stick. Cook until the vegetables are tender when pierced with the tip of a small knife, 25–30 minutes. Meanwhile, cook the remaining onions and fennel (see below).

3 COOK THE ONIONS AND FENNEL

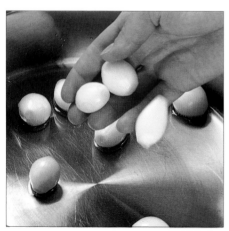

1 Heat the remaining vegetable oil and olive oil in the second sauté pan and sauté the rest of the baby onions, until lightly browned, about 3 minutes.

2 Put the second spice bag, remaining cooking liquid, and salt in the pan. Add the sliced fennel and bring the liquid to a fast boil over high heat.

3 Continue boiling, 10–12 minutes, then add the raisins to the fennel and onions in the sauté pan, and stir together to combine.

4 Continue boiling rapidly, stirring occasionally, and adding a little stock or water as the liquid evaporates. Cook until the onions and fennel are tender when pierced with the tip of a knife, 15–20 minutes. Remove the spice bags from both mixtures and taste for seasoning.

As cooking liquid reduces flavors are concentrated

🍴 **TO SERVE**

Serve the vegetable mixtures in separate bowls at room temperature. Decorate the fennel with a sprig of parsley, and the mushrooms with a sprig of fresh thyme, if you like.

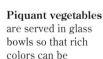

Piquant vegetables are served in glass bowls so that rich colors can be appreciated

Cooking liquid is aromatic with coriander, peppercorns, bay leaf, parsley, and thyme

GOLDEN GREEK-STYLE VEGETABLES

1 Omit the mushrooms, fennel, and raisins. Make the spice bags as directed, using ⅓ cup coriander seeds, 1½ tbsp black peppercorns, 4 bay leaves, 9–12 sprigs of fresh coriander (cilantro), and 6–9 sprigs of parsley.
2 Prepare the cooking liquid, the tomatoes, and baby onions as directed. Trim the florets from 1 small head cauliflower (weighing about 1½ lb), cutting the florets in half if large. Wash and trim 2 medium zucchini (total weight about 1 lb) and cut them into ¼-inch slices. Soak a large pinch of saffron in a little boiling water.
3 Heat 2 tbsp vegetable oil and 2 tbsp olive oil in each of 2 sauté pans. Divide the baby onions between the 2 pans. Add the cauliflower, a spice bag, half of the cooking liquid, half of the saffron with its liquid, and salt to a pan.
4 Put the zucchini in the other pan with a spice bag, the tomatoes, the remaining cooking liquid, saffron with its liquid, and salt.
5 Cook the vegetables until tender, 25–30 minutes, adding more stock or water as necessary.
6 Serve in separate bowls, decorating the cauliflower with a bay leaf, and the zucchini with coriander leaves, if you like.

SMOKED TROUT MOUSSE WITH HORSERADISH AND DILL

🍽 SERVES 8–10 🥣 WORK TIME 20–25 MINUTES*

EQUIPMENT

1¹/₂-quart terrine mold with lid

chef's knife

small knife

bowls

rubber spatula

whisk†

pastry brush

small saucepan

chopping board

†electric mixer can also be used

ANNE SAYS
"If using a mold made from a metal such as aluminum or tin, do not store the mousse in it longer than 4 hours, or it will discolor the mousse and taint the flavor."

INGREDIENTS

smoked trout

fresh horseradish†

fresh dill

watercress

lemon juice

eggs

plain yogurt

heavy cream

bottled mayonnaise

powdered unflavored gelatin

scallions

†bottled horseradish can be used

ORDER OF WORK

1 PREPARE THE INGREDIENTS

2 MAKE THE MOUSSE

3 UNMOLD THE MOUSSE

Made with flaked, smoked trout in a mayonnaise base lightened with yogurt, this mousse is a refreshing start to any meal. I sometimes use a fish-shaped mold for a more festive presentation.

GETTING AHEAD
The mousse can be prepared up to 1 day ahead and kept, covered, in the refrigerator.
plus 3–4 hours chilling time

SHOPPING LIST

2	eggs
3	small scallions
1	small bunch of fresh dill
2	smoked trout, total weight about 1¹/₂ lb
	vegetable oil for mold
1 tbsp	powdered unflavored gelatin
¹/₄ cup	cold water
¹/₂ cup	bottled mayonnaise
¹/₂ cup	plain yogurt
3 tbsp	grated fresh horseradish, more to taste
	juice of 1 lemon
	salt and pepper
³/₄ cup	heavy cream
1	bunch of watercress for serving

1 PREPARE THE INGREDIENTS

1 Put the eggs in the saucepan, cover with cold water, and bring to a boil. Simmer 10 minutes. Drain the eggs, let cool in a bowl of cold water. Tap the eggs to crack the shells, peel them, and rinse with cold water. Coarsely chop the eggs.

Egg adds texture to mousse

Egg should be coarsely chopped

Hold egg with your fingertips as you chop

2 Trim the scallions and finely slice them, including the trimmed green tops.

4 Remove the skin from the smoked trout by peeling it off with the help of the small knife. Then carefully lift off the fish fillets from the bones; discard the heads, bones, and skin.

Skin separates easily from flesh of smoked trout

3 Strip the dill leaves from the stems and pile them on the chopping board. With the chef's knife, finely chop the leaves.

5 Holding the fillets in 1 hand, flake the trout flesh with a fork. Brush the mold with oil.

6 Sprinkle the gelatin over the cold water in a small bowl and let stand until the granules become spongy, about 5 minutes.

2 MAKE THE MOUSSE

1 Put the flaked trout, coarsely chopped eggs, scallions, dill, and mayonnaise in a medium bowl. Pour in the plain yogurt.

Plain yogurt has tart flavor that balances richness of smoked trout

Mayonnaise helps bind ingredients together

2 Add the horseradish, lemon juice, salt, and pepper and stir to blend the ingredients. Taste the mixture for seasoning.

ANNE SAYS
"The mousse should be well seasoned."

3 Whip the cream in a chilled bowl until soft peaks form when the whisk is lifted, 3–5 minutes.

Rubber spatula is good for smoothing top of mousse

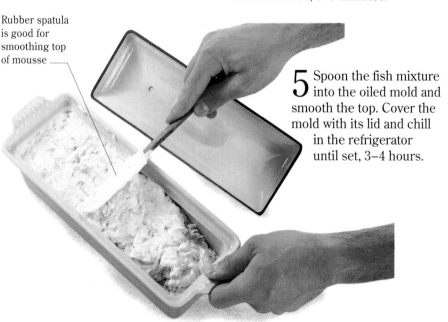

5 Spoon the fish mixture into the oiled mold and smooth the top. Cover the mold with its lid and chill in the refrigerator until set, 3–4 hours.

4 Melt the gelatin in the small saucepan over low heat. Add it to the trout mixture and mix very thoroughly. At once, fold in the whipped cream.

! TAKE CARE !
Work quickly because the gelatin will set rapidly if the trout mixture is cold.

3 UNMOLD THE MOUSSE

1 Run the small knife around the edges of the mold. Dip the base of the mold in a bowl of warm water for a few seconds to loosen the mousse, then wipe the base of the mold dry.

ANNE SAYS
"Use the back of the knife to avoid cutting into the mousse mixture."

2 Set a platter on top of the mold and invert so that the mousse falls onto the platter.

Mold comes off easily after dipping in warm water

 **TO SERVE**
Cut the mousse into ³/₄-inch slices and set a slice on each plate. Decorate each serving with 1–2 sprigs watercress.

Crisp watercress leaves are pleasant contrast to creamy texture of mousse

Flaked smoked trout and chopped egg give texture to mousse

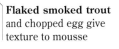

SMOKED TROUT MOUSSE WITH GREEN PEPPERCORNS

This spicy mousse combines green peppercorns with the smoked fish.

1 Omit the scallions, dill, and horseradish. Rinse and drain 1¹/₂ tbsp green peppercorns.
2 Make the mousse as directed, adding the green peppercorns and the juice of ¹/₂ lemon to the fish mixture. Fill the terrine mold and chill it until set, as directed in the main recipe.
3 Prepare a cucumber garnish: peel 1 cucumber with a vegetable peeler, or peel it in strips with a citrus stripper, if you like. Cut the cucumber into very thin slices. With a small knife, make a slit to the center of each slice.
4 Unmold the mousse and cut it into ³/₄-inch slices. Set a slice on each plate.
5 Twist each cucumber slice so it sits upright and use to decorate the servings, with lemon sections and flat-leaf parsley, if you like.

BLINI WITH SMOKED SALMON

EQUIPMENT

metal bowl

whisk

saucepans

chef's knife

small knife

large skillet †

heatproof plate

bowls

metal spatula

strainer   ladle

rubber spatula

wooden spoon

† griddle can also be used

INGREDIENTS

smoked salmon

red onion   capers

milk

all-purpose flour

butter

radishes

buckwheat flour

eggs

sour cream

active dry yeast

Blini are pancakes of Russian origin, with a lightness and a nutty flavor given by buckwheat flour. They are usually served with smoked salmon or caviar and condiments such as chopped radishes, onions, and capers. A bowl of sour cream is the mandatory accompaniment, with melted butter, too, if you like.

*plus 2–3 hours standing time

SHOPPING LIST

1 cup	milk, more if needed
1½ tsp	active dry yeast or ½ cake (9 g) compressed yeast
¼ cup	lukewarm water
½ cup	all-purpose flour
¾ cup	buckwheat flour
½ tsp	salt
2	eggs
¼ cup	butter, more if needed
2 tbsp	sour cream
	For the condiments
1	small red onion
2–3 tbsp	drained capers
8	red radishes
6 oz	sliced smoked salmon
¾ cup	sour cream for serving
½ cup	butter for serving (optional)

ORDER OF WORK

1 MAKE THE BLINI BATTER

2 PREPARE THE CONDIMENTS

3 FINISH BATTER; COOK THE BLINI

1 MAKE THE BLINI BATTER

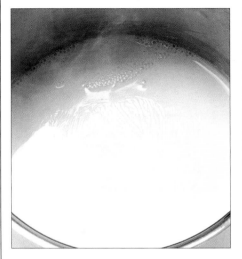

1 Pour three-quarters of the milk into a saucepan and bring just to a boil over medium heat. Let the milk cool to lukewarm.

2 Meanwhile, sprinkle or crumble the yeast over the lukewarm water in a small bowl and let stand until dissolved, about 5 minutes.

3 Sift the all-purpose flour with the buckwheat flour and salt into a large bowl. Using your fingers, make a well in the center.

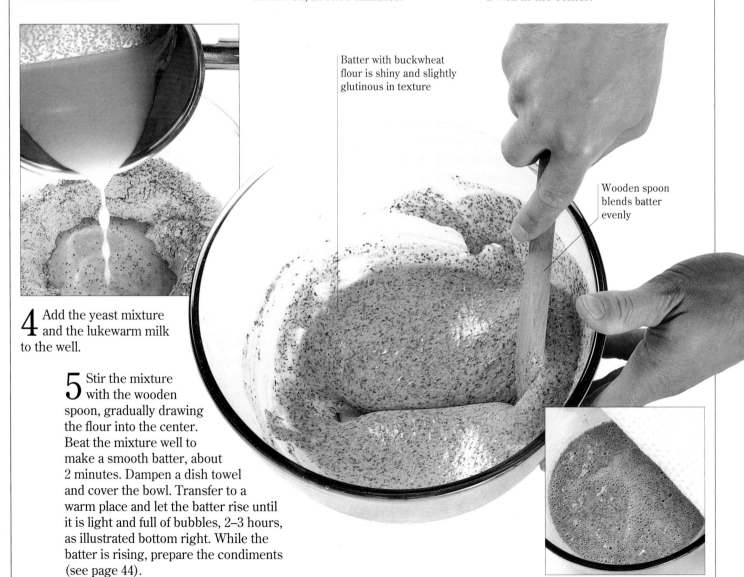

Batter with buckwheat flour is shiny and slightly glutinous in texture

Wooden spoon blends batter evenly

4 Add the yeast mixture and the lukewarm milk to the well.

5 Stir the mixture with the wooden spoon, gradually drawing the flour into the center. Beat the mixture well to make a smooth batter, about 2 minutes. Dampen a dish towel and cover the bowl. Transfer to a warm place and let the batter rise until it is light and full of bubbles, 2–3 hours, as illustrated bottom right. While the batter is rising, prepare the condiments (see page 44).

2 PREPARE THE CONDIMENTS

1 Peel the red onion, leaving the root attached, and cut it lengthwise in half. Slice each half horizontally toward the root, but not through it.

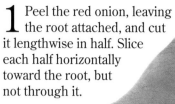

Leave some root to hold onion layers together

2 Slice the onion vertically, again leaving the root end uncut. Finally, cut across the onion to make dice. Continue chopping the onion until it is very fine. Put the chopped onion in a small serving bowl.

3 Coarsely chop the drained capers if they are large. Transfer them to a small serving bowl.

Discard papery onion skins

4 Trim the roots and tops from the radishes. Wash, dry, then thinly slice the radishes.

Fold smoked salmon slices for attractive presentation

5 Put the sliced radishes in a small serving bowl. Cover the radishes, onions, and capers, and set aside until ready to serve.

6 Arrange the slices of smoked salmon on a serving plate, cover and keep in the refrigerator.

3 FINISH BATTER; COOK THE BLINI

1 Heat the oven to low for keeping the blini warm. Separate the eggs. Melt half of the butter in a small saucepan and cool slightly. Pour the remaining milk into the risen batter and stir until mixed.

2 Stir in the egg yolks, melted butter, and sour cream. Add more milk if necessary so the batter is the consistency of heavy cream.

Egg yolks enrich batter

For stiff texture, always use metal bowl when whisking egg whites

3 Put the egg whites into the metal bowl and beat with the whisk until stiff peaks form when the whisk is lifted, 3–5 minutes.

! TAKE CARE !
Do not overbeat the egg whites or they will become grainy.

4 Add about one-quarter of the beaten egg whites to the blini batter and gently stir with the rubber spatula until thoroughly mixed.

Rubber spatula makes folding easy by cutting through egg whites and batter

5 Pour the batter and egg-white mixture into the remaining beaten egg whites.

6 Fold the mixtures together: cut down into the center of the bowl with the rubber spatula, scoop under the contents and turn them over in a rolling motion. At the same time, with your other hand, turn the bowl counter-clockwise. Continue folding until the batter is thoroughly blended.

7 Heat half of the remaining butter in the skillet. Pour in the batter with a small ladle to make several 3-inch rounds.

ANNE SAYS
"Do not overcrowd the blini in the pan."

Batter will spread slightly on hot skillet

8 Cook until the undersides of the blini are lightly browned and the tops are bubbling, 1–2 minutes. Turn them over and brown the other side.

9 Transfer the blini to the heatproof plate, overlapping them so they remain moist, and keep warm in the heated oven. Continue to make blini, adding more butter to the pan as needed.

Smoked salmon is a colorful and tasty accompaniment to blini

BLINI WITH RED AND BLACK CAVIAR

Choose lumpfish or beluga sturgeon caviar, depending on your budget.

1 Make the blini batter as directed. Omit the red onion, capers, radishes, and smoked salmon.
2 Hard-boil 2 eggs. Peel the eggs, then separate the yolks and whites; finely chop them both. Trim 2 scallions and cut the green tops into thin diagonal slices. Finish the batter and cook the blini as directed. Serve them with 1 oz each red and black caviar (or more to taste), chopped egg yolks and egg whites, scallion slices, and a spoonful of sour cream.

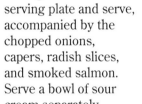 **TO SERVE**
Melt the butter, if using. Arrange the blini on a serving plate and serve, accompanied by the chopped onions, capers, radish slices, and smoked salmon. Serve a bowl of sour cream separately, and a bowl of melted butter if you like.

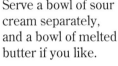

Traditional assortment of condiments accent the nutty flavor of blini

GETTING AHEAD
The bowls of condiments can be prepared up to 2–3 hours ahead and kept tightly covered. The blini are best cooked at the last minute, although they can be made up to 8 hours ahead and warmed in a low oven just before serving.

Marinated
Goat Cheese Salad

Salade de Chèvre Mariné

   SERVES 8 · WORK TIME 20–25 MINUTES* · COOKING TIME 5–8 MINUTES

EQUIPMENT

large glass jar with lid †

slotted spoon

whisk

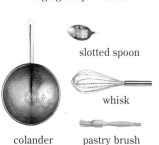

colander · pastry brush

small knife

metal spatula

strainer

bowl · salad bowl

paper towels · 3-inch cookie cutter

baking sheet

† shallow non-metallic bowl and plastic wrap can also be used

A glass jar of little goat cheeses, marinating in herbs, chili peppers, and golden oil, is an eye-catcher in any kitchen. The marinating oil is used in the dressing.

*plus 1 week marinating time

SHOPPING LIST

8	slices of whole-wheat bread
For the marinated goat cheeses	
4	round goat cheeses, weighing about 2–3 oz each, firm but not dry, or 1 goat cheese log, weighing about 11 oz
2	bay leaves
2–3	sprigs of fresh thyme
2–3	sprigs of fresh rosemary
2–3	sprigs of fresh oregano
2 tsp	black peppercorns
2	small dried hot red chili peppers
2 cups	olive oil, more if needed
For the vinaigrette	
5–7	sprigs of fresh thyme
2 tbsp	red wine vinegar
1 tsp	Dijon-style mustard
	salt and pepper
For the salad	
2	heads of Belgian endive, weighing about 6 oz each
1	head of red-leaf lettuce, weighing about ½ lb

INGREDIENTS

goat cheese

whole-wheat bread

Belgian endive

red-leaf lettuce

fresh thyme

olive oil · red wine vinegar · bay leaves

peppercorns · dried chili peppers

Dijon-style mustard

fresh oregano

fresh rosemary

ORDER OF WORK

1 MARINATE THE CHEESES

2 MAKE THE VINAIGRETTE AND PREPARE THE SALAD

3 MAKE THE GOAT CHEESE TOASTS

1 MARINATE THE CHEESES

1 Put the goat cheeses in the large glass jar with the bay leaves, the 2–3 sprigs of thyme, rosemary, and oregano, the peppercorns, and chili peppers. Add enough olive oil to cover generously.

2 Cover the jar with its lid and leave the goat cheeses at least 1 week before using.

ANNE SAYS
"If using a goat cheese log, put it in a non-metallic bowl with the other ingredients, cover with plastic wrap, and marinate 1–3 days only."

Fragrant herbs add flavor to olive oil marinade

2 MAKE THE VINAIGRETTE AND PREPARE THE SALAD

1 Remove the goat cheeses from the marinade with the slotted spoon, draining off any excess oil.

Oil from marinating cheeses adds depth of flavor to vinaigrette

2 Strain the oil. You will need 6 tbsp for the vinaigrette and a little more for the bread.

ANNE SAYS
"Any remaining oil can be kept and used for other dressings."

3 Strip the leaves from the 5–7 thyme sprigs. Whisk the vinegar in the bowl, with the mustard, salt, and pepper. Gradually whisk in 6 tbsp strained olive oil so the vinaigrette emulsifies and thickens slightly.

4 Stir in half of the thyme. Taste for seasoning and adjust if necessary.

5 Wipe the endive heads with a damp paper towel, trim the stems, and discard any discolored leaves. Separate the remaining leaves.

6 Wash the red-leaf lettuce under cold running water, discarding the tough stems, and drain the leaves well in the colander.

7 Put the endive leaves in the salad bowl and tear the lettuce leaves into pieces as you add them; toss gently with your hands.

3 MAKE THE GOAT CHEESE TOASTS

2 Using the cookie cutter, cut out a round from each slice of whole-wheat bread.

1 Heat the oven to 400° F. Cut each goat cheese in half horizontally.

ANNE SAYS
"If using a goat cheese log, cut it into 8 equal slices."

Bread trimmings can be made into breadcrumbs and frozen for future use

3 Set the bread rounds on the baking sheet and brush with a little of the strained olive oil. Bake in the heated oven until lightly toasted, 3–5 minutes.

Rounds should be slightly larger in diameter than cheese

Cheese will melt and spread over bread

4 Heat the broiler. Put a piece of cheese on top of each toasted bread round. Broil until the cheese is bubbling and golden, 2–3 minutes.

🍽 TO SERVE

Toss the salad greens with the vinaigrette and arrange the salad on individual plates. Place the cheese toasts on the salads and sprinkle with the remaining thyme. Serve immediately.

Fresh thyme tastes good with goat cheese

Hot cheese toasts contrast with cool, crisp salad

V A R I A T I O N

BREADED MARINATED GOAT CHEESE SALAD

1 Marinate the goat cheeses as directed in the main recipe.
2 Make the vinaigrette as directed.
3 Omit the endive. Trim the stems from 1 bunch of watercress, wash, and drain. Prepare 1 red-leaf lettuce and combine with the watercress.
4 Put ¹/₃ cup flour on a sheet of waxed paper. Lightly beat 1 egg and 1 large pinch of salt in a shallow bowl. Put ¹/₂ cup dried breadcrumbs on another sheet of paper. Coat the marinated goat cheese halves with the flour, then dip them in the beaten egg, and finally coat with the breadcrumbs. Use 2 forks to turn the cheeses.
5 Heat 1 tbsp butter in a frying pan with 1 tbsp oil from the marinade and sauté the cheese slices, in 2 batches, until lightly browned and crisp, 1–2 minutes on each side. Add 1 tbsp more butter and 1 tbsp more oil before frying the second batch.
6 Toss the salad with the vinaigrette and pile on individual plates. Serve the hot cheese on the side.

GETTING AHEAD

Individual goat cheeses can be marinated 3–4 weeks in the refrigerator, but will soften if kept too long. Do not marinate softer goat cheese logs more than 3 days. Make the cheese toasts and assemble the salad just before serving.

Spring Rolls with Lettuce and Mint Leaves

EQUIPMENT

wok †

bowls

chef's knife

pastry brush

metal spatula

whisk

colander

small knife

strainer

heatproof plate

citrus juicer

paper towels

chopping board

tongs

metal skewer

† large frying pan can also be used

A wrapping of crisp iceberg lettuce and mint leaves, added by guests at the table, wonderfully lightens the Asian treat of fried spring rolls.

*plus 30 minutes soaking time

INGREDIENTS

iceberg lettuce

fresh mint

spring roll wrappers

cellophane noodles

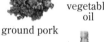

ground pork

vegetable oil

garlic cloves

honey

fish sauce

limes

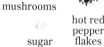

dried shiitake mushrooms

sugar

hot red pepper flakes

egg

onion

ANNE SAYS

"Egg roll wrappers are thicker than spring roll wrappers and easier to use."

ORDER OF WORK

1   MAKE THE FILLING

2   ASSEMBLE ROLLS

3   PREPARE LETTUCE; MAKE THE SAUCE

4   FRY THE ROLLS

SHOPPING LIST

16	spring or egg roll wrappers, defrosted if frozen
1	egg
1	medium head of iceberg lettuce
1/2 cup	vegetable oil for frying, more if needed
1	medium bunch of fresh mint
	For the filling
1 oz	dried shiitake or other oriental mushrooms
2 oz	cellophane noodles
1	medium onion
2	garlic cloves
2 tbsp	vegetable oil
8 oz	ground pork
3 tbsp	Asian fish sauce (nam pla or patis)
1 tsp	sugar
	ground black pepper
	For the hot red pepper dipping sauce
6	garlic cloves
2	limes
1 cup	water
1/2 cup	Asian fish sauce
1	pinch of hot red pepper flakes
1/4 cup	honey

1 MAKE THE FILLING

1 Soak the dried mushrooms in a bowl of warm water until plump, about 30 minutes. Meanwhile, soak the cellophane noodles in a second bowl of warm water until softened, about 15 minutes.

Dried mushrooms have robust flavor

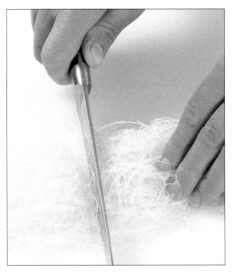

Warm water softens brittle cellophane noodles

2 Drain the noodles and cut them across into about 2-inch lengths. Drain the mushrooms and finely chop them.

ANNE SAYS
"Once the noodles are soaked they are easily cut into pieces."

3 Peel the onion, leaving a little of the root attached, and cut it lengthwise in half. Slice each half horizontally, leaving the slices attached at the root end, then slice vertically.

4 Finally, cut across the onion to make dice. Continue chopping the onion until it is fine.

Stir garlic constantly so it browns evenly

Garlic becomes fragrant as it cooks

5 Set the flat side of the chef's knife on top of each garlic clove and strike it with your fist. Discard the skin and finely chop the garlic.

6 Heat the oil in the wok, add the garlic, and cook, stirring, until fragrant, 30 seconds.

Keep stirring to combine ingredients and prevent sticking

7 Add the chopped onion to the wok and continue stir-frying until softened, 1–2 minutes.

8 Add the pork and cook, stirring, until brown, 3–5 minutes. Stir in the mushrooms, cellophane noodles, fish sauce, sugar, and black pepper, and taste for seasoning.

Cellophane noodles are soft enough to blend with pork and mushrooms

2 ASSEMBLE ROLLS

Push filling onto wrapper with fingertip

1 Lay a damp dish towel on the work surface. Set the spring roll wrappers on half of the towel and fold the other half on top to keep them moist. Lightly beat the egg.

ANNE SAYS
"Egg roll wrappers do not need to be kept moist. Simply spread them on the work surface."

Arrange filling on wrapper so it forms neat cylinder when rolled

2 Set a wrapper on a work surface with a corner facing toward you. If using spring roll wrappers, replace the damp dish towel on top of the remaining wrappers. Put 1–2 spoonfuls of filling on the lower half of the wrapper.

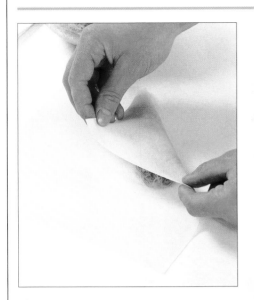

3 Fold the bottom corner of the wrapper up and over the filling.

Spring roll wrappers tear easily so handle carefully

4 Using the pastry brush or your finger, moisten the side corners with beaten egg. Fold the sides over to cover the bottom corner and the filling, and press firmly to seal.

5 Brush the top open corner of the wrapper with a little of the beaten egg to seal the spring roll.

6 Hold the wrapper steady with both hands and roll it up into a cylinder shape.

Beaten egg holds spring roll wrapper together

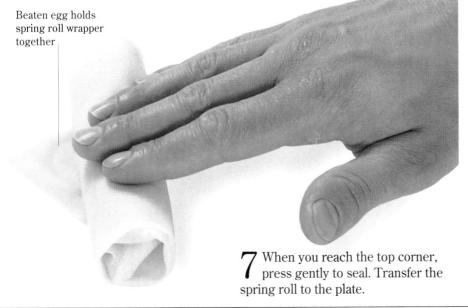

7 When you reach the top corner, press gently to seal. Transfer the spring roll to the plate.

8 Repeat with the remaining wrappers and filling, placing the sealed rolls on a plate; set aside.

3 PREPARE LETTUCE; MAKE THE SAUCE

1 Cut the core from the lettuce with the small knife. Hold the lettuce, core upward, under cold running water, so the force of the water separates the leaves. There should be at least 16 leaves. Wash the leaves and shake them dry.

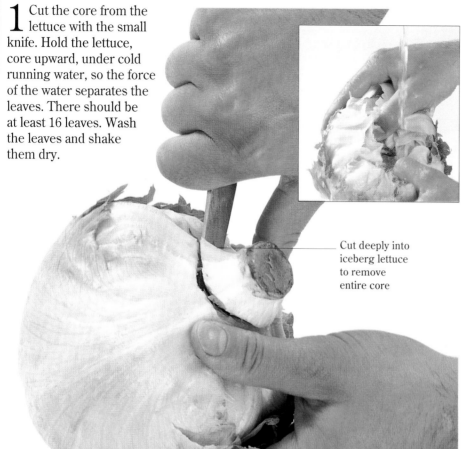

Cut deeply into iceberg lettuce to remove entire core

Hold lettuce firmly while cutting out core

2 Wrap the lettuce in damp paper towels and keep in the refrigerator while you are frying the spring rolls.

3 Peel and finely chop the garlic. Squeeze the limes. There should be 1/3 cup juice. In a bowl, combine the garlic, lime juice, water, fish sauce, and hot red pepper flakes. Add the honey.

4 FRY THE ROLLS

2 During frying, turn the spring rolls until they are evenly browned and the filling is warm.

1 Heat the oven to low to keep spring rolls warm. Heat the vegetable oil in the wok. Fry the spring rolls in batches, 3–5 minutes. Add more oil, if necessary, between batches.

Tongs grasp spring rolls for easy turning

Skewer tests if spring rolls are done

Batch of 3 spring rolls fits neatly in wok

3 To test that the filling is cooked, insert the skewer in a roll. The skewer should feel warm when withdrawn after 30 seconds.

4 Transfer the spring rolls to the heatproof plate lined with paper towels to drain. Keep warm in the oven.

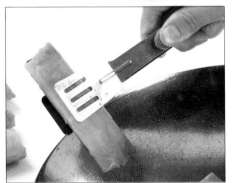

🍽 TO SERVE

Arrange lettuce leaves and mint leaves on each individual plate. Divide the spring rolls among the plates. Serve with a small bowl of sweet-sour sauce for dipping.

To eat a spring roll, wrap it in a lettuce leaf with 1–2 mint leaves and dip it in sauce

VARIATION
SPRING ROLLS FILLED WITH SHRIMP

1 Omit the lettuce and mint from the main recipe. Make a carrot salad: shred 6 peeled carrots in a food processor or on a coarse hand grater. In a medium bowl, combine $1/2$ cup water, 1 tbsp cider vinegar, 1 tbsp sugar, and $1/2$ tsp salt; add the carrots. Let stand at least 1 hour to marinate.

2 Meanwhile, make the filling: prepare the mushrooms, cellophane noodles, onion, and garlic as directed. Omit the pork. Chop 8 oz peeled and cooked shrimp. With a small knife, peel the skin from $1/2$-inch piece of fresh ginger root. With a chef's knife, slice the ginger, cutting across the fibrous grain. Crush each slice of ginger with the flat of the knife, then finely chop the slices.

3 Heat the garlic and ginger in the oil. Add the onion and stir-fry until softened, 1–2 minutes. Add the shrimp and stir-fry about 30 seconds. Add the other filling ingredients as directed.

4 Make the hot red pepper sauce as directed in the main recipe.

5 Assemble and fry the spring rolls as directed. Serve them with the sauce, and the well-drained carrot salad.

GETTING AHEAD

The dipping sauce can be made up to 8 hours ahead and kept refrigerated; add the hot red pepper flakes not more than 1 hour ahead so the sauce is not too hot. The spring rolls can be assembled up to 8 hours ahead and kept, covered, in the refrigerator. Fry them just before serving.

STUFFED MUSHROOMS WITH HERBS

🍽 SERVES 4   🥣 WORK TIME 25–30 MINUTES   🍲 BAKING TIME 15–20 MINUTES

EQUIPMENT

chef's knife

pastry brush

small knife

frying pan

wooden spoon

cheese grater

paper towels

medium baking dish

bowls

chopping board

Stuffed mushrooms are hard to beat. These are filled with chopped wild mushrooms and walnuts, perfumed with garlic and plenty of herbs.

GETTING AHEAD

The mushrooms can be stuffed up to 4 hours ahead and kept, covered, in the refrigerator. Bake them in a 350° F oven, 15–20 minutes.

SHOPPING LIST

12	large mushrooms, total weight about 1 lb
3–4 tbsp	grated Parmesan cheese
	For the stuffing
3 oz	fresh wild mushrooms such as shiitake or oyster mushrooms, or ¾ oz dried wild mushrooms
12–14	sprigs of fresh tarragon
10–12	sprigs of fresh chervil
7–10	sprigs of fresh thyme
¾ cup	walnut halves or pieces
3	garlic cloves
¼ cup	olive oil, more for baking dish
	juice of ½ lemon
	salt and pepper
6 tbsp	heavy cream

INGREDIENTS

large mushrooms

fresh wild mushrooms

fresh tarragon

fresh thyme

fresh chervil †

lemon juice

Parmesan cheese

garlic cloves

olive oil

walnuts

heavy cream

† parsley can also be used

ORDER OF WORK

1 PREPARE THE MUSHROOMS AND STUFFING

2 STUFF AND BAKE THE MUSHROOMS

1 PREPARE THE MUSHROOMS AND STUFFING

1 Pull out the stems from the large mushrooms, leaving the caps whole for stuffing. Wipe the caps with damp paper towels. Trim the stems.

Remove stems carefully so caps do not break

Mushroom caps are ideal containers for stuffing

2 Wipe the fresh wild mushrooms and trim the stems. If using dried mushrooms, soak them in hot water until plump, about 30 minutes. Drain them and cut into pieces.

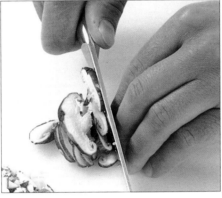

3 Slice the wild mushrooms and large mushroom stems, then stack the slices, and cut across to make dice. Finely chop the dice. Alternatively, chop the mushrooms in a food processor, taking care not to overwork them or they will form a purée.

Tarragon, chervil, and thyme flavor mushroom stuffing

4 Set aside 4 sprigs of each herb for garnish. Chop the remaining herbs (see box, right). Combine one-quarter of the chopped herbs with the Parmesan cheese and set aside for the topping.

HOW TO CHOP FRESH HERBS

Tarragon, rosemary, chervil, parsley, dill, basil, chives, thyme, and basil are herbs that are usually chopped before being combined with other ingredients. Delicate herbs such as basil bruise easily; do not chop them too finely.

Leaves are pulled from woody stems

1 Strip the leaves or sprigs from the stems. Pile the leaves or sprigs on a chopping board.

2 Cut the leaves or sprigs into small pieces with a chef's knife. Holding the tip of the blade against the board and rocking the blade back and forth, continue chopping the herbs.

ANNE SAYS
"When using a large quantity of herbs, or sprigs of herbs, hold them in a bunch while chopping."

Herb trio lends distinctive flavor

5 Coarsely chop the walnuts. Set the flat side of the chef's knife on top of each garlic clove and strike it with your fist. Discard the skin and finely chop the garlic.

Walnuts add crunchy texture to stuffing

6 Heat half of the oil in the frying pan. Add the chopped mushrooms and garlic with the lemon juice, salt, and pepper. Cook, stirring, until all the liquid has evaporated, 3–5 minutes. Stir in the heavy cream and cook until slightly thickened, 1–2 minutes. Add the walnuts and chopped herbs and stir to mix. Taste for seasoning.

2 STUFF AND BAKE THE MUSHROOMS

Mound stuffing in mushrooms because it will shrink slightly during baking

Seasoned mushroom caps are ready for tasty stuffing

1 Heat the oven to 350° F. Lightly oil the baking dish. Season the mushroom caps with salt and pepper. Spoon 1–2 tbsp stuffing into each mushroom cap, mounding it well. Set the stuffed mushrooms in the prepared baking dish.

Grated Parmesan
will brown attractively
when stuffed mushrooms
are baked

2 Sprinkle about 1 tsp of
the Parmesan and herb
topping on each stuffed mushroom.
Spoon the remaining oil evenly over the
mushrooms. Bake in the heated oven until the
mushroom caps are tender when pierced with
a knife and the filling is very hot, 15–20 minutes.

🍴 TO SERVE

Serve the mushrooms on a
platter or on individual plates.
Garnish with herbs, and
additional walnuts,
if you like.

Stuffing with wild mushrooms
and crunchy walnuts is enhanced
by cheese and herb topping

V A R I A T I O N

MUSHROOMS STUFFED WITH SUN-DRIED TOMATOES AND CHEESE

*Savory sun-dried tomatoes are
combined with two different
cheeses in this stuffing.*

1 Omit the wild mushroom and herb
stuffing; chop only 3–5 sprigs each of
fresh tarragon and chervil or parsley.
2 Prepare the large mushrooms
as directed in the main recipe,
discarding the stems.
3 Dice 2 oz mozzarella cheese.
4 Drain ¼ cup (about 2 oz)
oil-soaked sun-dried tomatoes
and put them in a food
processor with 4 peeled garlic
cloves and ⅔ cup creamy
ricotta cheese. Work the
ingredients to a purée.
Alternatively, chop the sun-
dried tomatoes and garlic
finely by hand with a chef's
knife, then combine them
with the cheese.
5 Transfer the mixture to a
bowl and stir in the chopped
herbs and diced mozzarella.
Season the stuffing to taste with
salt and pepper.
6 Stuff the mushrooms with the
tomato-cheese mixture. Sprinkle
with ¼ cup grated Parmesan
cheese, dividing it equally among
the mushrooms. Sprinkle with oil
and bake as directed.

CHEESE PUFFS WITH SPINACH AND SMOKED SALMON

Gougères Farcies

🍽️ SERVES 8 🥣 WORK TIME 40–45 MINUTES 🍲 BAKING TIME 30–35 MINUTES

EQUIPMENT

saucepans

chef's knife

pastry brush

frying pan

bowls

strainer

wire rack

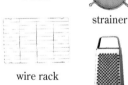
metal spatula   grater

serrated knife

wooden spoon

2 baking sheets

chopping board

Cheese puffs are traditional in Burgundy, where they are displayed in almost every bakery window. Here they are filled with spinach and smoked salmon for a more modern touch. Needless to say, a glass of white Burgundy wine is the perfect accompaniment.

SHOPPING LIST

For the choux pastry	
1 cup	flour
7 tbsp	unsalted butter, more for baking sheets
4 oz	Gruyère cheese
1 cup	water
1¼ tsp	salt
5–6	eggs
For the spinach and smoked salmon filling	
1	medium onion
4	garlic cloves
2 lb	fresh spinach
6 oz	smoked salmon
½ lb	cream cheese
2 tbsp	butter
1	pinch of ground nutmeg
	salt and pepper
¼ cup	milk

INGREDIENTS

smoked salmon

fresh spinach†   cream cheese

onion

milk

garlic cloves

butter   ground nutmeg

eggs   Gruyère cheese

flour

†defrosted spinach can also be used

ORDER OF WORK

1 MAKE THE CHOUX PASTRY DOUGH

2 GLAZE AND BAKE THE CHEESE PUFFS

3 MAKE THE FILLING AND FILL THE PUFFS

1 MAKE THE CHOUX PASTRY DOUGH

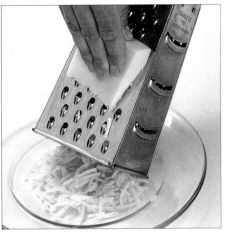

1 Sift the flour into a medium bowl. Melt a little butter and brush it over both of the baking sheets. Heat the oven to 375°F.

2 Using the coarse side of the grater, grate the Gruyère cheese onto a plate and set aside. Cut the 7 tbsp butter into small pieces.

3 Melt the butter in a medium saucepan with the water and ³/₄ tsp salt. Bring just to a boil.

! TAKE CARE !
The butter must melt before the water boils or the evaporation will change the dough proportions.

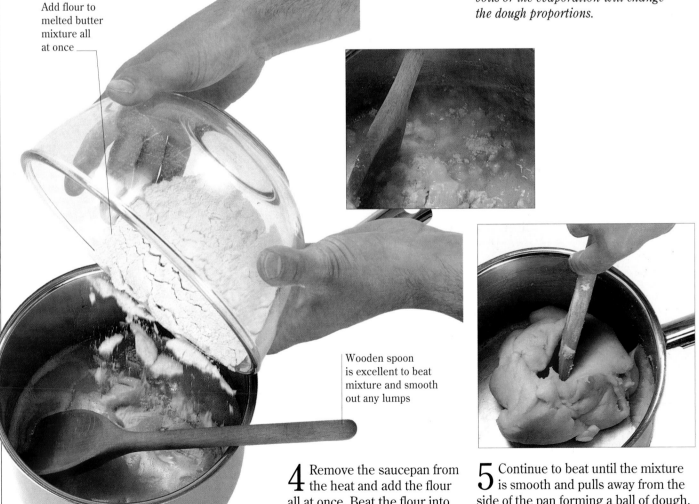

Add flour to melted butter mixture all at once

Wooden spoon is excellent to beat mixture and smooth out any lumps

4 Remove the saucepan from the heat and add the flour all at once. Beat the flour into the butter mixture vigorously with the wooden spoon.

5 Continue to beat until the mixture is smooth and pulls away from the side of the pan forming a ball of dough, about 1 minute. Return the pan to the stove and beat over very low heat to dry out the dough, about 30 seconds.

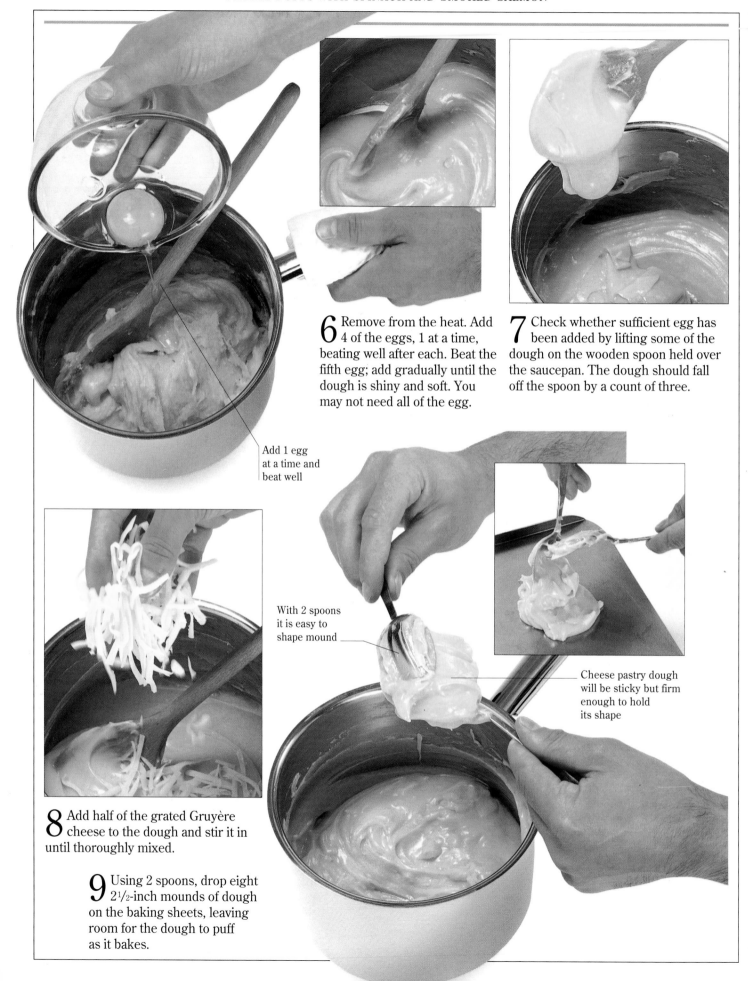

Add 1 egg
at a time and
beat well

6 Remove from the heat. Add 4 of the eggs, 1 at a time, beating well after each. Beat the fifth egg; add gradually until the dough is shiny and soft. You may not need all of the egg.

7 Check whether sufficient egg has been added by lifting some of the dough on the wooden spoon held over the saucepan. The dough should fall off the spoon by a count of three.

With 2 spoons
it is easy to
shape mound

Cheese pastry dough
will be sticky but firm
enough to hold
its shape

8 Add half of the grated Gruyère cheese to the dough and stir it in until thoroughly mixed.

9 Using 2 spoons, drop eight 2½-inch mounds of dough on the baking sheets, leaving room for the dough to puff as it bakes.

2 GLAZE AND BAKE THE CHEESE PUFFS

1 Make the egg glaze: lightly beat the remaining egg with the remaining ½ tsp salt in a small bowl. Brush some glaze over each of the choux puffs.

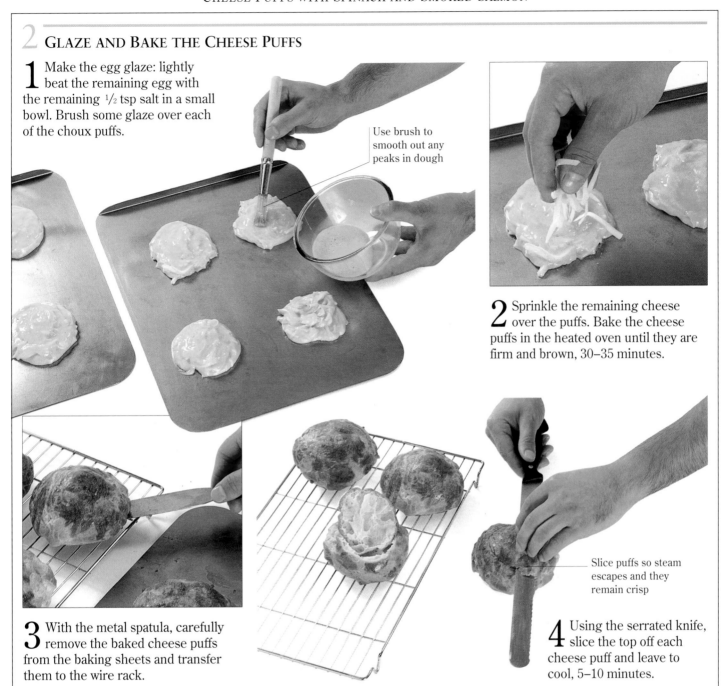

Use brush to smooth out any peaks in dough

2 Sprinkle the remaining cheese over the puffs. Bake the cheese puffs in the heated oven until they are firm and brown, 30–35 minutes.

3 With the metal spatula, carefully remove the baked cheese puffs from the baking sheets and transfer them to the wire rack.

Slice puffs so steam escapes and they remain crisp

4 Using the serrated knife, slice the top off each cheese puff and leave to cool, 5–10 minutes.

3 MAKE THE FILLING AND FILL THE PUFFS

1 Peel the onion, leaving a little of the root attached, and cut it lengthwise in half. Lay each onion half cut-side down on the chopping board and slice horizontally toward the root, leaving the slices attached at the root end. Then slice vertically, again leaving the root end uncut. Finally, cut across the onion to make dice.

2 Set the flat side of the chef's knife on top of each garlic clove and strike it with your fist. Finely chop the garlic.

3 Discard the tough ribs and stems from the fresh spinach, then wash the leaves thoroughly.

Remove stringy spinach stems before cooking

4 Bring a large saucepan of salted water to a boil. Add the spinach, and simmer until tender, 1–2 minutes.

5 Drain the spinach, rinse with cold water, and drain again. Squeeze the cooked spinach or defrosted spinach to remove excess water, then finely chop.

Holding knife with both hands speeds up chopping

6 Slice the smoked salmon into ¼-inch x 3-inch strips. Cut the cream cheese into cubes.

7 Melt the butter in the frying pan. Add the onion and cook until soft but not brown, 3–5 minutes. Add the garlic, and nutmeg, salt, pepper to taste, and the spinach. Continue cooking, stirring occasionally, until any liquid from the spinach has evaporated, 5 minutes longer.

8 Add the cream cheese and stir until melted and the mixture is thoroughly combined. Remove the frying pan from the heat.

9 Add two-thirds of the smoked salmon, and pour in the milk. Stir thoroughly, heat through 1–2 minutes, then taste for seasoning.

Milk moistens spinach mixture

Smoked salmon cooks slightly in hot mixture

10 Mound 2–3 tbsp filling in each cheese puff. Arrange the remaining strips of smoked salmon in a lattice on top.

🍽 TO SERVE

Place a cheese puff on each of 8 individual plates. Rest the lid against the side of each filled puff and serve immediately.

Cheese-flavored choux pastry
forms crisp case

Smoked salmon lattice
makes attractive topping for spinach

V A R I A T I O N

CHEESE RINGS FILLED WITH SPINACH AND MUSHROOMS

Mushrooms take the place of smoked salmon in the spinach filling for these cheese rings.

1 Make the choux pastry as directed. Fit a pastry bag with a ³/₈-inch plain tube. Fill the bag with the choux pastry.
2 Pipe out a 4-inch diameter ring onto a buttered baking sheet. Pipe out a second ring directly on top of the first. Repeat to make 8 rings. Brush the rings with egg glaze and bake as directed.
3 Make the filling: omit the smoked salmon. Wipe ³/₄ lb mushroom caps with damp paper towels, trim the stems even with the caps, and thinly slice the caps. Cook the onions as directed, add the mushrooms with the garlic, and sauté until the mushrooms are tender, about 5 minutes; reserve some mushroom slices to garnish the tops of the rings, if you like. Add the spinach to the pan and finish the filling as directed.
4 Using a serrated knife, slice the baked rings in half. Set a cheese ring on each individual plate. Spoon the filling into the bottom half of each ring and set the upper half on top. Garnish the cheese rings with mushroom slices, if reserved.

GETTING AHEAD

The dough and filling can be made up to 6 hours ahead and kept in the refrigerator. Bake the puffs not more than 1 hour ahead. Reheat the spinach mixture and fill the puffs just before serving.

POACHED SCALLOPS IN CIDER SAUCE

🍴 SERVES 6   🥄 WORK TIME 45–50 MINUTES   🍲 BROILING TIME 2–3 MINUTES

EQUIPMENT

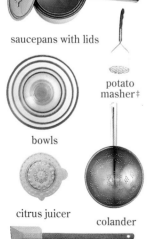

food processor †

6 scallop
half-shells

filleting knife

chef's knife

small knife

whisk

slotted spoon

wooden spoon

small strainer

pastry brush

vegetable
peeler

pastry bag with
medium star tube

saucepans with lids

potato
masher ‡

bowls

citrus juicer

colander

rubber spatula

† blender can also be used

‡ potato ricer can also be used

A creamy cider sauce complements the sweet taste of scallops, which are served in half shells. Piped mashed potatoes flavored with garlic and herbs complete this pretty dish.

INGREDIENTS

scallops

sparkling
cider

shallots

lemons

garlic cloves

butter

dry white
wine

fresh tarragon

parsley

flour

egg

potatoes

heavy cream

egg yolks

SHOPPING LIST

1 lb	large sea or small bay scallops
2	shallots
2	lemons
½ cup	sparkling cider
1 cup	water
½ cup	dry white wine
2 tbsp	butter
2 tbsp	flour
2	egg yolks
½ cup	heavy cream
For the garlic-herb mashed potatoes	
1 lb	potatoes
	salt and pepper
4–6	sprigs of parsley
4–6	sprigs of fresh tarragon
2	garlic cloves
4 tbsp	butter
2	egg yolks
For the egg glaze	
1	egg
½ tsp	salt

ORDER OF WORK

1 PREPARE AND PIPE THE GARLIC-HERB MASHED POTATOES

2 PREPARE AND POACH THE SCALLOPS

3 MAKE THE CIDER SAUCE

4 FINISH THE DISH

1 PREPARE AND PIPE THE GARLIC-HERB MASHED POTATOES

1 Peel the potatoes and cut each one into 2–3 pieces. Put them in a saucepan of cold salted water, cover, and bring to a boil. Simmer until the potatoes are tender, 15–20 minutes.

2 Meanwhile, strip the parsley and tarragon leaves from the stems. Peel the garlic cloves.

Herbs, butter, and garlic will enrich mashed potato

Food processor makes puréeing butter very easy

3 Put the butter, garlic, and herb leaves in the food processor. Purée until the garlic and herbs are finely chopped.

Tender potatoes will mash easily

Fork pierces potatoes easily when they are fully cooked

4 To test if the potatoes are tender, pierce them with a fork; they should feel soft. Drain the potatoes, then return them to the pan.

5 Carefully mash the potatoes with the potato masher, making sure no lumps remain.

Beat egg yolks into potatoes off heat so yolks cook gradually

6 Beat the herb purée into the potatoes over low heat until the potatoes are smooth, 2–3 minutes. Remove from the heat and beat in the egg yolks, one at a time. Season with salt and pepper. Let cool slightly.

7 Spoon the potatoes into the pastry bag fitted with the star tube. When full, twist the top until there is no air left in the bag.

8 Pipe the mashed potatoes in rosettes around the edge of each scallop shell.

ANNE SAYS
"Alternatively, spread the potatoes around the shells, making peaks with a fork."

Egg glaze will turn potato rosettes golden brown when brushed over and broiled

9 Make the egg glaze: lightly beat the egg and salt together. Brush the egg glaze on the potato borders. Set the scallop shells in a broiler pan.

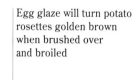

Colorful piped potatoes nestle in upward curve of scallop shell

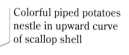

2 PREPARE AND POACH THE SCALLOPS

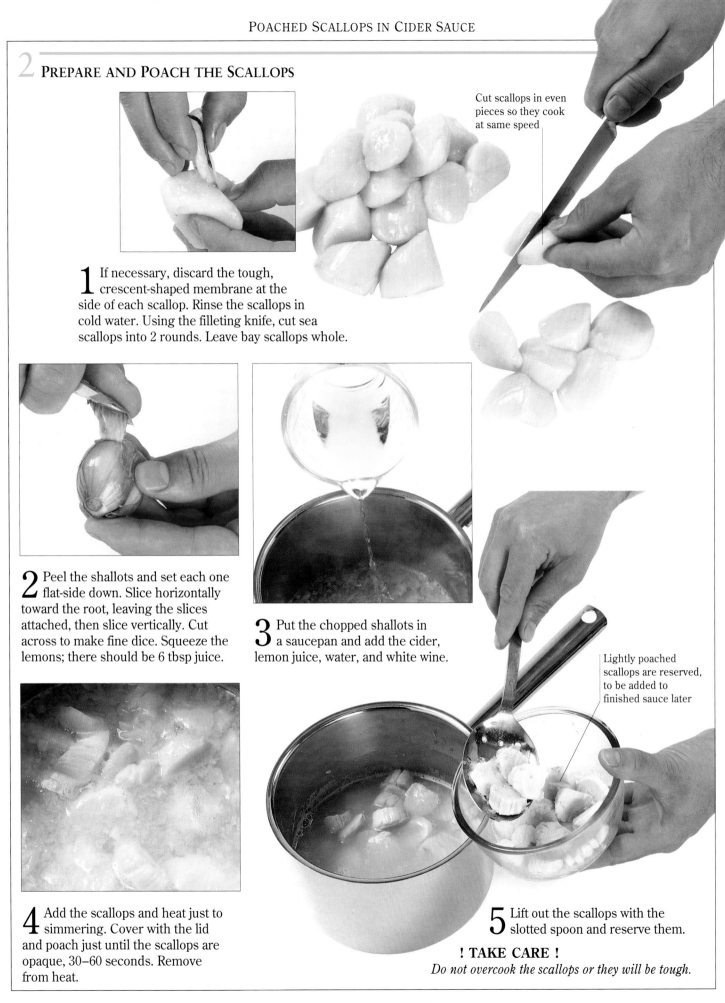

Cut scallops in even pieces so they cook at same speed

1 If necessary, discard the tough, crescent-shaped membrane at the side of each scallop. Rinse the scallops in cold water. Using the filleting knife, cut sea scallops into 2 rounds. Leave bay scallops whole.

2 Peel the shallots and set each one flat-side down. Slice horizontally toward the root, leaving the slices attached, then slice vertically. Cut across to make fine dice. Squeeze the lemons; there should be 6 tbsp juice.

3 Put the chopped shallots in a saucepan and add the cider, lemon juice, water, and white wine.

Lightly poached scallops are reserved, to be added to finished sauce later

4 Add the scallops and heat just to simmering. Cover with the lid and poach just until the scallops are opaque, 30–60 seconds. Remove from heat.

5 Lift out the scallops with the slotted spoon and reserve them.

! TAKE CARE !
Do not overcook the scallops or they will be tough.

3 MAKE THE CIDER SAUCE

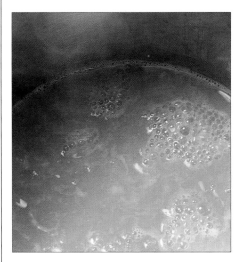

1 Return the pan of scallop cooking liquid to the heat and bring to a boil. Simmer until it is reduced to about 1 cup. Take the pan from the heat.

Whisk constantly so flour and butter do not scorch

When mixture foams remove from heat and continue whisking

2 Melt the butter in another saucepan. Whisk in the flour and cook until the mixture foams, 30–60 seconds.

3 Take the pan from the heat, cool slightly, then strain the reduced cooking liquid into it and whisk to mix.

4 Return to the heat and cook, whisking constantly, until the sauce boils and thickens, 1 minute longer. Take the pan from the heat.

Hot sauce will be enriched by egg yolks and cream

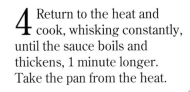

5 In a small bowl, whisk together the egg yolks and cream, then add a few spoonfuls of the hot sauce and whisk to mix. Whisk this mixture back into the pan of sauce.

6 Return the pan to low heat and cook just until the sauce thickens slightly, 1–2 minutes.

! TAKE CARE !
Do not let the sauce boil or it will curdle.

4 FINISH THE DISH

1 Heat the broiler. Add the reserved, poached scallops to the sauce with any liquid in the bowl. Taste the sauce for seasoning and adjust if necessary.

Shells are natural containers for poached scallops in sauce

Scallop shells filled on broiler pan can be transferred easily to broiler

2 Spoon the scallop and sauce mixture into the shells, inside the border of potato rosettes. Broil 3–4 inches from the heat, until the potatoes and scallops are very hot and browned, 2–3 minutes.

🍴 TO SERVE
Transfer the scallop shells to a platter or individual plates and serve immediately.

Potato rosettes form pretty border around scallop shells

V A R I A T I O N

SAUTEED SCALLOPS WITH LEMON-HERB POTATOES

1 Prepare the mashed potatoes as directed, omit the garlic and egg yolks and beat in the grated zest of 1 lemon with the herb butter. Cover the mashed potatoes with ⅓ cup milk and set in a water bath to keep warm.
2 Heat the oven to low for keeping the scallops warm. Clean the scallops as directed, but do not poach them (omit the cider sauce). Put 4–6 tbsp flour on a sheet of waxed paper and season with salt and pepper. Roll the scallops in the flour and pat them to discard excess.
3 Heat 2 tbsp butter and 2 tbsp oil in a frying pan. Sauté the scallops, turning them once, until brown and just crisp, 2–3 minutes. Transfer to a heatproof plate and keep warm in the oven.
4 Stir the milk into the potatoes; if still too thick, add 2–3 tsp more milk.
5 Using 2 tablespoons, shape the mashed potatoes into quenelles: scoop out a spoonful of potatoes, then shape into a neat, three-sided oval by turning the spoons against one another.
6 Arrange 3 quenelles on each of 6 individual plates, leaving the center open for a scallop; omit the egg glaze.
7 Divide the scallops among the plates and serve at once, with lemon wedges for decoration.

--- GETTING AHEAD ---
The potatoes, scallops, and sauce can be prepared and assembled in the shells up to 8 hours ahead; keep covered and refrigerated. Broil just before serving, to heat thoroughly.

HERBED SALMON CAKES WITH CORN RELISH

EQUIPMENT

food processor†

baking dish

citrus juicer

heatproof plate

vegetable peeler

chef's knife

frying pans

small knife

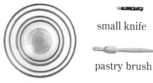
bowls

pastry brush

metal spatula

paper towels

whisk

aluminum foil

wooden spoon

large metal spoon

chopping board

† blender can also be used

The delicate, rich flesh of salmon is easily transformed into cakes, served here with tangy corn relish. This recipe is an excellent way to use up leftover cooked fish.

*plus 2–4 hours standing time

SHOPPING LIST

	butter for baking dish and foil
2	lemons
2 lb	fresh salmon fillets
¾ cup	fish stock or water, more if needed
4	slices of white bread
1	small bunch of parsley
1	small bunch of fresh dill
¼ cup	bottled mayonnaise
2	eggs
¼ cup	vegetable oil
	salt and pepper
	For the corn relish
1	medium onion
1	celery stalk
1	green bell pepper
2½ cups	corn kernels, defrosted or drained canned
½ cup	olive oil
1 tbsp	sugar
1 tsp	mustard powder
⅓ cup	red wine vinegar

INGREDIENTS

salmon fillets†

corn kernels

fish stock

dill

celery

vegetable oil

parsley

olive oil

eggs

white bread

lemons

red wine vinegar

mustard powder

butter

sugar

bottled mayonnaise

bell pepper

onion

† four 7¾ oz cans salmon can also be used

ORDER OF WORK

1 MAKE THE CORN RELISH

2 MAKE THE SALMON CAKE MIXTURE

3 SHAPE AND COOK THE SALMON CAKES

1 MAKE THE CORN RELISH

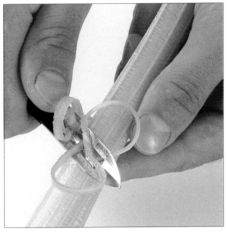

1 Peel the onion, leaving a little of the root attached, and cut it lengthwise in half. Lay each onion half flat on the chopping board and slice horizontally, then vertically toward the root, leaving the slices attached at the root end. Finally cut across to make dice.

2 Peel the strings from the celery stalk with the vegetable peeler. Cut the celery stalk across into thin slices.

3 Dice the bell pepper (see box, right). Put the corn, onion, and celery in a large bowl, and add the bell pepper. Combine the ingredients thoroughly, using the large metal spoon.

Hold corner of chopping board over bowl and scrape with back of knife to transfer chopped vegetables easily

For relish, vegetables should be cut in even-sized dice

HOW TO CORE AND SEED A BELL PEPPER AND CUT IT INTO STRIPS OR DICE

The cores and seeds of bell peppers are always discarded.

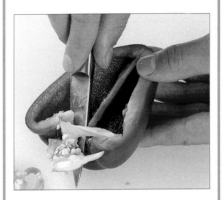

1 Cut around the pepper core and pull it out. Halve the pepper lengthwise and scrape out the seeds. Cut away the white ribs on the inside of the pepper.

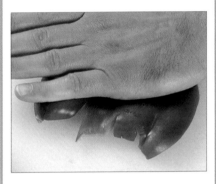

2 Set each pepper half cut-side down on a work surface and press down with the heel of your hand to flatten it.

3 With a chef's knife, slice the pepper half lengthwise into strips. For dice, gather the strips together in a pile and cut across into squares.

4 Put the oil, sugar, and mustard powder in a medium bowl with salt and pepper. Pour in the vinegar.

Red wine vinegar adds bite to relish dressing

Dressing will flavor relish ingredients

5 Whisk the dressing ingredients together and pour over the vegetable mixture.

6 Toss the vegetables in the dressing until thoroughly mixed. Season to taste. Cover and let stand at room temperature, to allow the flavors to mellow, 2–4 hours.

2 MAKE THE SALMON CAKE MIXTURE

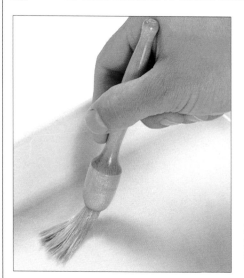

Paper towels pat salmon dry

1 Heat the oven to 350° F. Melt the butter and grease the baking dish. Squeeze the juice from 1 of the lemons.

2 Remove the skin from the salmon fillets, then rinse the salmon in cold water and pat dry.

Surface of salmon is white from sprinkling of lemon juice

3 Arrange the fillets in a single layer in the dish. Sprinkle the salmon with the lemon juice, salt, and pepper. Add enough of the fish stock or water to half cover the fillets.

4 Brush a little butter over a piece of foil and use to cover the salmon. Poach the salmon fillets in the heated oven, 15–20 minutes.

Herbs will enhance flavor of salmon cakes

5 Meanwhile, trim and discard the crusts from the white bread. Put the bread slices in the food processor and work to form crumbs.

6 Strip the parsley and dill leaves from the stems, and pile them on the chopping board. With the chef's knife, coarsely chop the leaves.

7 Test if the salmon is cooked: it should just flake easily when pierced with a fork. Remove the salmon from the oven; reduce the oven temperature to low.

8 Drain the salmon, and let cool slightly. Flake the fillets using 2 forks. Pick over the salmon with your fingers, making sure that there are no small bones. Transfer the flaked salmon to a large bowl.

Stir gently with wooden spoon so salmon remains in flakes

10 Stir the salmon mixture gently but thoroughly with the wooden spoon so the ingredients are combined.

9 Add the mayonnaise, herbs, and breadcrumbs to the salmon. Season with salt and pepper.

11 Lightly beat the eggs. Add them to the salmon cake mixture and stir to combine.

12 To test for seasoning, heat 1 tbsp oil in the frying pan, and fry a little piece of the salmon mixture until brown on both sides. Taste, then adjust the seasoning of the remaining mixture if necessary.

3 SHAPE AND COOK THE SALMON CAKES

1 Divide the salmon cake mixture into 16 portions. Roll each portion into a ball, wetting your hands if the mixture is sticky. Flatten each ball into a cake, about ½-inch thick.

Use wet hands to roll portions if mixture is sticky

! TAKE CARE !
Work gently when shaping the salmon mixture so the cakes will be light.

2 Heat the remaining oil in the frying pan. Add a batch of salmon cakes to fill the frying pan without overcrowding. Fry the salmon cakes over medium-high heat until they are golden, 3–4 minutes. Carefully turn the cakes over with the metal spatula and brown them on the other side.

3 Line the heatproof plate with paper towels, and transfer the cooked salmon cakes to the plate to drain. Keep them warm in the oven while cooking the remaining cakes. Cut the second lemon into wedges for serving.

Paper towels absorb excess oil after frying salmon cakes

Salmon cakes served at once are crisp on the outside and moist in the center

Relish adds crisp finish to salmon cakes

🍽 TO SERVE
Divide the corn relish between 8 plates and serve 2 salmon cakes on top of each, with a lemon wedge, and a decoration of celery leaves, if you like.

VARIATION
MARYLAND CRAB CAKES

When we had a summer house in Maryland, we made these cakes with local blue crabs. Fresh crabmeat is ideal, but expensive; canned crab works well too.

1 Prepare the corn relish as directed, replacing the green bell pepper with a red bell pepper.
2 Omit the salmon fillets. Pick over 2 lb lump crabmeat with your fingers, discarding any cartilage or shell. Prepare the crab mixture as for the salmon cakes. Divide the mixture into 16 portions.

3 Shape the crab cakes, about 1/2-inch thick. Fry them as directed.
4 Serve 2 crab cakes per person with the corn relish. Decorate with dill sprigs, if you like.

— GETTING AHEAD —
The corn relish can be prepared up to 4 days ahead and kept, covered, in the refrigerator. The salmon cakes can be shaped up to 4 hours ahead and refrigerated. Fry them just before serving.

STEAMED MUSSELS WITH SAFFRON-CREAM SAUCE

¶◎¶ SERVES 4–6 ⤸ WORK TIME 25–30 MINUTES 🍲 COOKING TIME 10–12 MINUTES

EQUIPMENT

large casserole with lid

whisk

chef's knife

colander

small knife

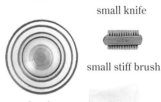
small stiff brush

bowls

cheesecloth

wooden spoon

medium saucepan

slotted spoon

large strainer

chopping board

aluminum foil

An echo from the shores of Brittany, these mussels are steamed with white wine, shallots, herbs, and saffron, just until the shells pop open. The natural juices of the mussels add rich flavor to the cooking liquid, which is thickened with cream to form a sumptuous sauce.

GETTING AHEAD

The mussels can be prepared 30 minutes ahead of serving and kept covered with foil. Just before serving, warm them in a 350°F oven, 2–3 minutes. Bring the sauce just back to a boil on top of the stove, coat the mussels, and serve.

SHOPPING LIST

3 quarts	mussels
3	shallots
1 cup	dry white wine
1	bouquet garni, made with 5–6 parsley stems, 2–3 sprigs fresh thyme, and 1 bay leaf
	1 large pinch of saffron threads
	salt and pepper
5–7	sprigs of parsley
½ cup	heavy cream

INGREDIENTS

mussels

shallots

bouquet garni

saffron threads

white wine

parsley

heavy cream

ANNE SAYS
"To save time, you can leave the mussels in both shells."

ORDER OF WORK

1 **PREPARE THE MUSSELS**

2 **COOK THE MUSSELS**

3 **MAKE THE SAUCE AND FINISH THE DISH**

1 PREPARE THE MUSSELS

Discard damaged mussels

1 Clean the mussels: scrub each one thoroughly under cold running water with the small stiff brush, then scrape using the small knife to remove any barnacles from the shell.

2 Discard any damaged mussels that have cracked or broken shells and those that do not close when tapped lightly on the work surface.

3 Detach and discard any weeds or "beards" from each mussel.

2 COOK THE MUSSELS

1 Peel the shallots and set each one flat-side down on the chopping board. Slice horizontally toward the root, leaving the slices attached. Slice vertically, again leaving the root end uncut, then cut across to make dice. Chop until very fine.

2 Put the wine, chopped shallots, bouquet garni, saffron threads, and plenty of pepper in the casserole. Bring to a boil and simmer 2 minutes.

Bouquet garni is tied to casserole handle

Mussels cook with very little liquid

3 Add the mussels to the casserole, cover, and cook over high heat, stirring occasionally, until the mussels open, 5–7 minutes.

! TAKE CARE !
Discard any mussels that have not opened once cooked.

Top mussel shells
are easily removed
and then discarded

4 Using the slotted
spoon, transfer
the mussels from the
cooking liquid to a
large bowl.

5 Discard the top
shell from each
mussel. Arrange each
mussel, in its bottom shell,
on a serving plate until all the
mussels are on the plate. Cover
tightly with foil and keep in a
warm place while making the
saffron-cream sauce.

Mussels look attractive
when arranged in circles
on very large plate

3 MAKE THE SAUCE AND FINISH THE DISH

Cheesecloth
finely strains
cooking
liquid

1 Strip the parsley leaves from
the stems and pile them on the
chopping board. With the chef's knife,
finely chop the leaves.

2 Set the strainer over the saucepan,
and line with the cheesecloth. Pour
the cooking liquid from the casserole
through the lined strainer into the pan.
Discard the bouquet garni.

3 Bring the cooking liquid to a boil,
and cook until reduced to 1/2 cup.
Pour the heavy cream into the reduced
cooking liquid.

4 Whisk in the cream, and bring back to a boil. Simmer the mixture until slightly thickened, stirring, 2–3 minutes. Allow to cool 1–2 seconds, then lift out the spoon and run your finger across – it should leave a clear trail. Stir in the chopped parsley. Season to taste.

🍴 **TO SERVE**
Remove the foil and spoon the saffron-cream sauce over the mussels.

VARIATION

MUSSELS STEAMED IN WHITE WINE

1 Prepare and cook the mussels in the wine and flavorings as directed.
2 Using a slotted spoon, transfer the mussels to individual soup bowls. Sprinkle with the chopped parsley.
3 Taste the cooking liquid for seasoning. Strain the cooking liquid as directed, and spoon it over the mussels. Serve at once.

VARIATION

CLAMS STEAMED IN WHITE WINE

A departure from the usual mussels, hard-shell clams are equally delicious steamed with white wine.

1 Scrub 4 quarts clams in place of the mussels; unlike mussels, clams do not have barnacles or weeds. Cook them as directed with shallots, white wine, and pepper, omitting the bouquet garni and saffron. Allow 7–10 minutes for the clams to open (thick shelled clams may take longer).
2 Serve the clams with the cooking liquid, leaving each guest to strip away any black membranes. You may like to serve the clams with a bowl of melted butter for dipping.

Saffron sauce
heightens orange tint of mussels

Chopped parsley
adds texture and vivid green highlights to mouthwatering mussels

SAUTEED ONION AND ROQUEFORT TART

🍽 SERVES 6–8 🥄 WORK TIME 40–50 MINUTES* 🍲 BAKING TIME 30–35 MINUTES

EQUIPMENT

scissors

10-inch tart pan

pastry scraper

pastry brush

frying pan with lid

ladle

chef's knife

chopping board

whisk

strainer

bowls

baking sheet

aluminum foil

rolling pin

wooden spoon

metal skewer

This is my version of a classic tart from Alsace. The filling of onions, cooked to melting softness, is baked in a tart shell with a little custard and flavored with piquant Roquefort cheese.

— GETTING AHEAD —

The tart is best freshly baked, but it can be made up to 1 day ahead and kept tightly covered in the refrigerator. Warm it in a 350° F oven 10–15 minutes before serving.

*plus 45 minutes chilling time

SHOPPING LIST

2–3	sprigs of fresh thyme
1 lb	onions
2 tbsp	unsalted butter, more for foil
	salt and pepper
6 oz	Roquefort cheese
	For the pie pastry dough
1²/₃ cups	flour, more for work surface
1	egg yolk
¹/₂ tsp	salt
3 tbsp	water, more if needed
7 tbsp	unsalted butter, more for tart pan
	For the custard
1	egg
1	egg yolk
¹/₂ cup	milk
	ground nutmeg
¹/₄ cup	heavy cream

INGREDIENTS

Roquefort cheese†

onions

heavy cream

fresh thyme

egg

egg yolks

butter

ground nutmeg

flour

milk

†other firm blue cheese can also be used

ORDER OF WORK

1 MAKE THE PIE PASTRY DOUGH

2 LINE THE TART PAN

3 BLIND BAKE THE PASTRY SHELL

4 PREPARE THE ONION FILLING AND BAKE THE TART

1 MAKE THE PIE PASTRY DOUGH

1 Sift the flour onto the work surface and make a well in the center. Put the egg yolk, salt, and water in the well.

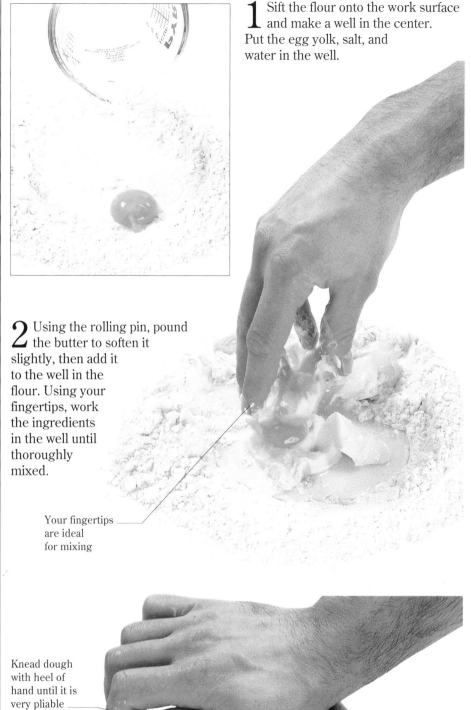

2 Using the rolling pin, pound the butter to soften it slightly, then add it to the well in the flour. Using your fingertips, work the ingredients in the well until thoroughly mixed.

Your fingertips are ideal for mixing

3 Draw in the flour with the pastry scraper. With your fingers, work the flour into the other ingredients until coarse crumbs form. Press the dough into a ball.

ANNE SAYS
"If the crumbs are dry, sprinkle them with more water before pressing the dough together."

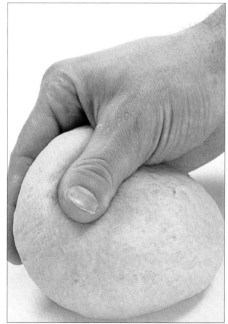

Knead dough with heel of hand until it is very pliable

4 Lightly flour the work surface, then blend the dough by pushing it away from you with the heel of your hand. Gather it up with the pastry scraper and continue to blend until it is very smooth and peels away from the work surface in 1 piece, 1–2 minutes.

5 Shape the dough into a ball, wrap it tightly, and chill until firm, about 30 minutes.

2 LINE THE TART PAN

Dough is easy to lift when wrapped around rolling pin

1 Butter the tart pan. Lightly flour the work surface. Roll out the chilled dough to a 12-inch round. Roll up the dough around the rolling pin and drape it over the pan, so that it hangs over the edge.

! TAKE CARE !
Be careful not to stretch the dough or it will shrink when baked.

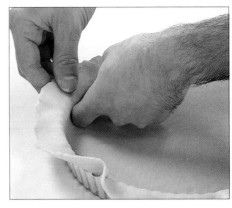

2 Gently lift the edge of the dough with 1 hand and firmly press it into the bottom edge of the pan with the forefinger of the other hand.

3 Roll the rolling pin over the top of the pan, pressing down to cut off the excess dough.

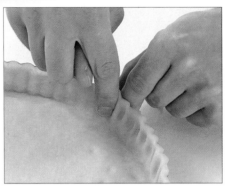

4 With your forefingers and thumb, press the dough evenly up the side, from the bottom, to increase the height of the dough rim.

5 Prick the bottom of the shell lightly with a fork to prevent air bubbles from forming during baking. Chill until firm, at least 15 minutes.

3 BLIND BAKE THE PASTRY SHELL

1 Heat the oven to 425° F. Line the pastry dough shell with a sheet of foil, pressing it well into the bottom edge. Trim the foil if necessary, using the scissors, so it stands about 1¹⁄₂ inches above the edge of the pan.

Foil helps dough keep its shape during baking

2 Half-fill the foil with chickpeas to weigh down the dough. Bake the pastry shell until set and starting to brown, about 15 minutes.

Chickpeas are used as "baking beans" to weigh down dough

Cover foil with even layer of chickpeas

3 Remove the foil and beans and reduce the oven temperature to 375°F. Continue baking until the pastry is lightly browned, 5–8 minutes longer. Remove the pastry shell from the oven and set aside; leave the oven on. Meanwhile, prepare the onion filling.

4 PREPARE THE ONION FILLING AND BAKE THE TART

1 Strip the thyme leaves from the stems and finely chop the leaves. Peel the onions, cut in half through root and stem, and slice thinly.

2 Melt the butter in the frying pan. Add the onions and chopped thyme and season with salt and pepper. Butter a piece of foil, press it on top of the onion mixture, and cover with the lid.

Replace foil and lid after each stirring

Onions should be soft enough to cut with wooden spoon

3 Cook over very low heat, stirring occasionally, until very soft but not brown, 20–30 minutes.

Ground nutmeg is excellent flavoring with Roquefort and onions

4 Meanwhile, make the custard: put the egg, egg yolk, milk, salt, pepper, and a pinch of ground nutmeg into a bowl. Pour in the heavy cream.

Cream adds richness to custard

5 Whisk the custard ingredients together until thoroughly mixed.

6 Crumble the Roquefort into a bowl, using your fingertips.

Heat of cooked onions melts Roquefort so mixture is creamy

7 Add the cheese to the softened onions; stir until melted and creamy. Let cool slightly. Using the back of the wooden spoon, spread the onion mixture evenly on the bottom of the pastry shell. Place the tart pan on a baking sheet.

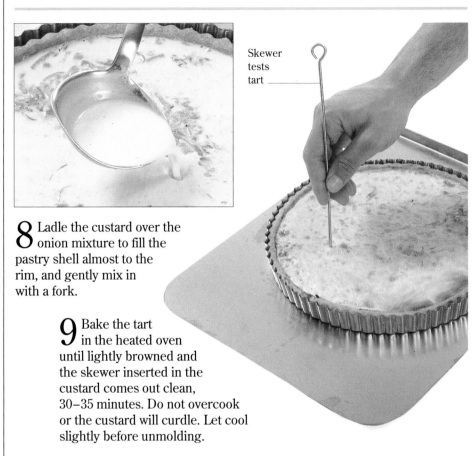

8 Ladle the custard over the onion mixture to fill the pastry shell almost to the rim, and gently mix in with a fork.

Skewer tests tart

9 Bake the tart in the heated oven until lightly browned and the skewer inserted in the custard comes out clean, 30–35 minutes. Do not overcook or the custard will curdle. Let cool slightly before unmolding.

🍴 TO SERVE

Remove the tart from the pan. Serve warm or at room temperature, cut in wedges. A salad of Belgian endive, watercress, and tomatoes makes a delicious accompaniment.

Crisp pastry
holds filling of sweet onions and creamy Roquefort cheese

VARIATION

CABBAGE AND GOAT CHEESE TART

This contemporary version of Sautéed Onion and Roquefort Tart is filled with green cabbage and creamy goat cheese. A soft fresh chèvre log works well, but you can use any type of goat cheese, or even feta if you like.

1 Make, line, and blind bake the tart shell as directed. Omit the onions. Shred 1/2 small green or Savoy cabbage (total weight about 1 1/2 lb): trim and discard any wilted leaves from the cabbage half. Cut a wedge around the core and remove it. Set the cabbage half cut-side down on a chopping board and finely shred it using a chef's knife. Discard any thick ribs. Cook the cabbage in butter as for the onions, taking care that it does not brown.

2 Make the custard as directed. Cut a 1/2-lb soft goat cheese log into 3/8-inch slices. Spread the shredded cabbage over the bottom of the tart shell and add the custard. Arrange the goat cheese rounds on top of the filling and bake the tart as directed.

ANNE SAYS
"If the cheese is not brown when the custard is set, brown it under the broiler, with a strip of foil over pastry edge."

OYSTERS IN CHAMPAGNE SAUCE

🍽 SERVES 4–6 🥣 WORK TIME 35–40 MINUTES 🍲 BROILING TIME 1–2 MINUTES

EQUIPMENT

saucepans

bowls

rubber spatula

large metal spoon

whisk

chef's knife

oyster knife

stiff brush

chopping board

The luxurious combination of fresh oysters with Champagne sauce, briefly broiled on the half shell, makes a rich, elegant first course. If you don't have an oyster knife, ask the fish store to open the oysters, making sure the juices are reserved for you.

GETTING AHEAD

The sauce can be made up to 30 minutes ahead and kept warm in the bowl, set in a large pan of warm, but not hot, water. Spoon the sauce over the oysters and broil the oysters just before serving.

INGREDIENTS

oysters

Champagne

egg yolks

lemon juice

shallots

butter

rock salt

ANNE SAYS
"Any type of oyster can be used, although the larger, deep-shelled varieties, such as Pacific oysters, are preferable. Crumpled foil can be used instead of rock salt to hold the oysters steady."

ORDER OF WORK

1 **PREPARE THE OYSTERS**

2 **MAKE THE CHAMPAGNE SAUCE**

3 **BROIL THE OYSTERS**

SHOPPING LIST

24	oysters in their shells
2½ lb	rock salt, about 4 cups, for holding oysters steady
	lemon wedges, parsley sprigs, and tomato strips for decoration (optional)
	For the Champagne sauce
4	shallots
¾ cup	butter
1½ cups	Champagne, about ½ bottle
4	egg yolks
	salt and pepper
	squeeze of lemon juice

1 PREPARE THE OYSTERS

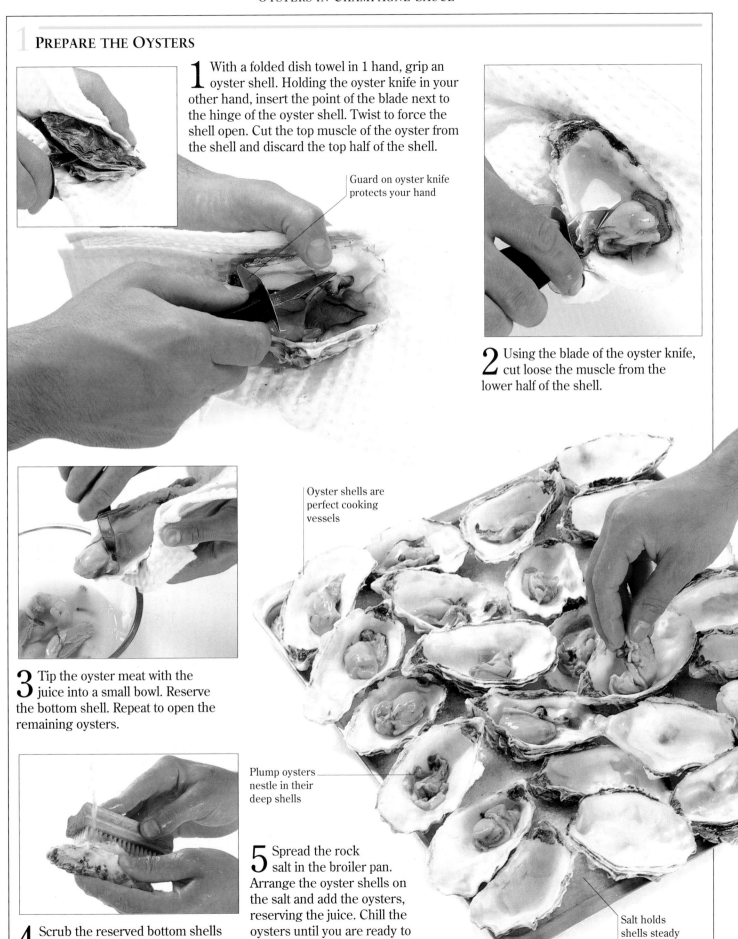

1 With a folded dish towel in 1 hand, grip an oyster shell. Holding the oyster knife in your other hand, insert the point of the blade next to the hinge of the oyster shell. Twist to force the shell open. Cut the top muscle of the oyster from the shell and discard the top half of the shell.

Guard on oyster knife protects your hand

2 Using the blade of the oyster knife, cut loose the muscle from the lower half of the shell.

Oyster shells are perfect cooking vessels

3 Tip the oyster meat with the juice into a small bowl. Reserve the bottom shell. Repeat to open the remaining oysters.

Plump oysters nestle in their deep shells

5 Spread the rock salt in the broiler pan. Arrange the oyster shells on the salt and add the oysters, reserving the juice. Chill the oysters until you are ready to broil them.

4 Scrub the reserved bottom shells clean under cold running water.

Salt holds shells steady in broiler pan

2 MAKE THE CHAMPAGNE SAUCE

1 Peel the shallots. Set each one flat-side down and slice horizontally toward the root, leaving the slices attached at the root. Slice vertically and cut across to make fine dice.

2 Melt the butter in a small pan. Skim the froth off the surface; take the pan from the heat and let cool.

3 Meanwhile, put the shallots in another small saucepan and add 1¼ cups Champagne. Boil until reduced to 2–3 tbsp. Let cool slightly.

4 Whisk together the egg yolks, oyster juice, and the Champagne mixture in a large heatproof bowl. Set the bowl over a pan of hot, but not boiling, water and whisk until very thick, 5–7 minutes. The mixture should form soft peaks and leave a ribbon trail when the whisk is lifted.

! TAKE CARE !
Do not overheat the sauce or it will curdle; it should thicken gradually.

Bowl should not touch water or sauce will overheat and may curdle

Whisk briskly so butter is emulsified with foaming egg mixture

5 Remove the pan from the heat and whisk the warm butter into the mixture in a slow, steady stream. Leave the milk solids from the butter at the bottom of the pan. Season the sauce with salt, pepper, and lemon juice. Whisk the remaining Champagne into the sauce.

! TAKE CARE !
If the butter is too hot or added too quickly, the sauce will separate.

3 BROIL THE OYSTERS

1 Heat the broiler. Spoon 1–2 tbsp sauce over each oyster. Broil the oysters about 4 inches from the heat until lightly browned, 1–2 minutes.

Oysters will be lightly cooked beneath creamy Champagne sauce

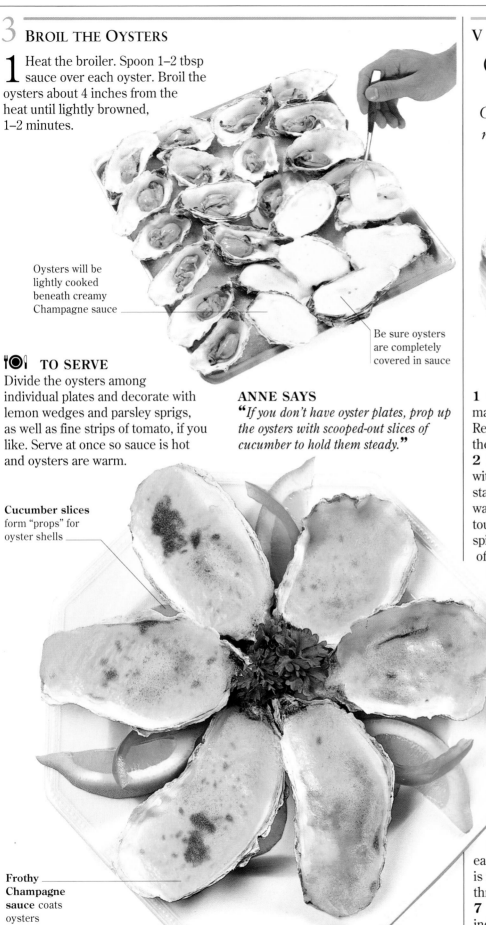

Be sure oysters are completely covered in sauce

TO SERVE

Divide the oysters among individual plates and decorate with lemon wedges and parsley sprigs, as well as fine strips of tomato, if you like. Serve at once so sauce is hot and oysters are warm.

ANNE SAYS
"If you don't have oyster plates, prop up the oysters with scooped-out slices of cucumber to hold them steady."

Cucumber slices form "props" for oyster shells

Frothy Champagne sauce coats oysters

OYSTERS ROCKEFELLER

This classic dish, from New Orleans, supposedly earned its name when it was proclaimed "as rich as Rockefeller".

1 Open the oysters as directed in the main recipe, discarding their liquid. Reserve them on their shells. Omit the Champagne sauce.

2 Peel the strings from 2 celery stalks with a vegetable peeler, then cut each stalk into 3–4 pieces. Thoroughly wash ¼ lb fresh spinach, discarding any tough stems, or use 3 tbsp defrosted spinach. Trim 3 scallions, leaving 1 inch of each green top, and cut them across into 3–4 pieces. Strip the leaves from 5–7 sprigs of parsley.

3 Work the celery, spinach, scallions, and parsley in a food processor until finely chopped. Transfer the vegetables to a bowl.

4 Trim and discard the crust from 1 slice of white bread. Work the bread in the food processor to form crumbs, then mix with the vegetables.

5 Add ¾ cup softened butter, ½ tsp Worcestershire sauce, a dash of Tabasco sauce, salt, and pepper, and combine until smooth.

6 Put 1 tbsp of the mixture on each oyster and broil until the butter is melted and the oysters are heated through, about 5 minutes.

7 Divide the oysters among individual plates and decorate with lemon wedges.

RED CABBAGE AND BACON SALAD WITH BLUE CHEESE

🍽 SERVES 6 🥄 WORK TIME 20–25 MINUTES*

EQUIPMENT

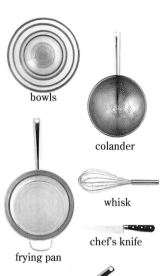

bowls

colander

whisk

chef's knife

frying pan

saucepans

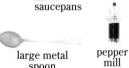

large metal
spoon

pepper
mill

wooden spatula

chopping board

INGREDIENTS

red cabbage

thick-cut bacon

romaine lettuce

red wine
vinegar

blue cheese

peppercorns   olive oil

Dijon-style mustard

ANNE SAYS
"If you prefer, you can use half olive oil and half vegetable oil when making the vinaigrette dressing."

Red cabbage with strips of bacon and crumbled blue cheese on a bed of lettuce makes a hearty first course for winter, or a tasty lunch for 4 people. I find the contrast in taste, texture, and color of peppery red cabbage, crunchy bacon, salty blue cheese, and crisp green lettuce especially good.

GETTING AHEAD

The vinaigrette dressing can be made up to 1 week ahead.
The cabbage can be prepared and tossed with
vinaigrette up to 2 hours before serving.

plus 1–2 hours marinating time

SHOPPING LIST

½ head	red cabbage (about 1½ lb)
¼ cup	red wine vinegar
2 quarts	boiling water
1	small head romaine lettuce
3 oz	blue cheese
½ lb	thick-cut bacon
	For the vinaigrette dressing
¼ cup	red wine vinegar, more if needed
1 tbsp	Dijon-style mustard
	salt and freshly ground black pepper
¾ cup	olive oil

ORDER OF WORK

1 **PREPARE THE VINAIGRETTE DRESSING**

2 **PREPARE THE CABBAGE**

3 **PREPARE THE REMAINING INGREDIENTS**

1 PREPARE THE VINAIGRETTE DRESSING

Pour oil in slow steady stream when making vinaigrette dressing

1 For the vinaigrette, combine ¼ cup vinegar with the mustard and a pinch of salt. Grind in pepper, to taste.

2 Gradually whisk in the oil so the vinaigrette emulsifies and thickens. Taste for seasoning.

ANNE SAYS
"I often make a bottle of dressing in advance and shake it just before using."

2 PREPARE THE CABBAGE

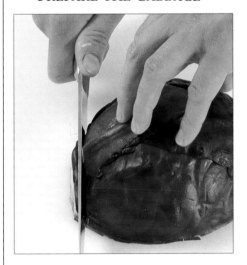

Cored cabbage is ready for shredding

Remove tough core from cabbage

1 Set the cabbage half cut-side down on the chopping board. Trim the stem end and discard. Peel off any outside leaves that are wilted.

2 Cut the cabbage lengthwise in half. Rest the stem end of 1 piece on the chopping board; cut out the core and discard. Repeat with the other piece.

3 Finely shred the cabbage quarters with the chef's knife, using your knuckles to guide the knife. Discard any thick ribs. Transfer the shredded cabbage to a large bowl.

4 Heat the vinegar to boiling in a small saucepan. Pour the vinegar over the shredded cabbage and toss to mix so it is thoroughly coated.

Cabbage turns magenta color after being tossed in hot vinegar and soaked briefly in boiling water

5 Pour the boiling water over the cabbage and let stand until slightly softened, 3–4 minutes. Drain thoroughly in the colander, then return it to the large bowl.

6 Toss the cabbage with enough vinaigrette to moisten it well. Taste for seasoning, adding more vinegar if necessary. Cover the bowl and marinate the cabbage in the dressing, 1–2 hours. Meanwhile, prepare the remaining ingredients.

3 PREPARE THE REMAINING INGREDIENTS

2 Remove and discard the thick stems from the lettuce. Stack the leaves and roll them up quite tightly. Cut the rolled lettuce leaves crosswise into wide strips.

1 Twist off and discard the root end from the lettuce. Discard any wilted leaves. Wash the lettuce well under cold running water, then drain the leaves thoroughly.

Lettuce leaves are easy to shred evenly when tightly rolled in cylinder

3 Crumble the blue cheese into a small bowl with your fingers, making sure that the pieces are not too small.

4 About ten minutes before serving the salad, stack the bacon slices and cut crosswise into strips. Cook the bacon in the frying pan, stirring occasionally, until crisp and the fat is rendered (melted), 3–5 minutes.

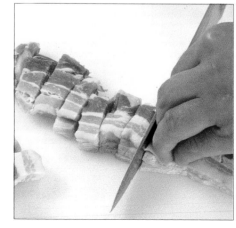

5 Spoon the hot bacon and pan juices over the red cabbage, reserving some bacon pieces for garnish. Toss them together.

Marinated cabbage will take on flavor from bacon

Bacon juices are added with crispy bacon pieces

6 Arrange a bed of shredded lettuce leaves on 6 individual plates. Spoon any remaining dressing over the lettuce. Mound the red cabbage and bacon mixture in the center.

🍴 **TO SERVE**
Top the salads with the blue cheese and reserved bacon, and serve at once.

Brilliant red cabbage is vivid background for crisp bacon and crumbled blue cheese

GREEN CABBAGE, WALNUT, AND BACON SALAD

Green cabbage takes the place of red, and the flavor and texture of walnuts add extra interest to the salad.

1 Make the vinaigrette dressing, substituting half walnut oil and half vegetable oil for the olive oil.
2 Omit the blue cheese. Prepare the romaine lettuce as directed. Shred ½ head green cabbage (about 1½ lb) as for the red cabbage. Omit the vinegar. Cover with the boiling water and let stand until softened, 3–4 minutes. Drain, rinse with warm water, and drain again thoroughly.
3 Coarsely chop ¾ cup walnuts, reserving some walnut halves for garnish, if you like.
4 Combine the cabbage and the walnuts, then toss with the vinaigrette. Prepare the bacon as directed, pour it over the cabbage with the pan juices, and toss at once. Garnish with the walnut halves, if reserved, and serve on a bed of shredded lettuce leaves.

SZECHUAN SWEET AND SOUR SPARERIBS

🍽 SERVES 6   ⏱ WORK TIME 15–20 MINUTES   🍲 COOKING TIME 1½ HOURS

EQUIPMENT

wok

bowls

small knife

tongs   boning knife

whisk

chopping board

INGREDIENTS

spareribs   sesame oil

vegetable oil   chili paste †

honey   dark soy sauce

scallions

dry sherry   cider vinegar

dried hot red chili pepper

† dried hot red pepper flakes can also be used

Spareribs are appreciated around the world. In this recipe, they are first browned in a chili-flavored oil, then slowly simmered until tender, and coated in a delectable sauce. To make spareribs a main course for 4 people, serve with boiled or fried rice.

GETTING AHEAD

The spareribs can be cooked up to 1 day ahead and kept, covered, in the refrigerator. Reheat the ribs in a 350°F oven, 10–15 minutes.

SHOPPING LIST

¼ cup	dark soy sauce
¼ cup	cider vinegar
3 tbsp	honey
1 tbsp	sesame oil
1 tsp	chili paste
¼ cup	dry sherry
1	bunch of scallions for decoration
3 lb	spareribs
¼ cup	vegetable oil
1	dried hot red chili pepper
1 quart	water, more if needed

ORDER OF WORK

1 PREPARE THE SWEET AND SOUR SAUCE AND GARNISH

2 TRIM AND COOK THE SPARERIBS

1 PREPARE THE SWEET AND SOUR SAUCE AND GARNISH

1 In a small bowl, whisk together the dark soy sauce, cider vinegar, honey, sesame oil, chili paste, and dry sherry. Make the scallion brushes (see box, right).

Sweet and sour sauce will give rich oriental flavor to spareribs

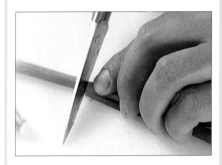

Aromatic flavors will permeate spareribs

2 TRIM AND COOK THE SPARERIBS

Loose flap of meat is easily removed with sharp knife

1 Using the boning knife, trim any loose flaps of meat and the excess fat from around the spareribs.

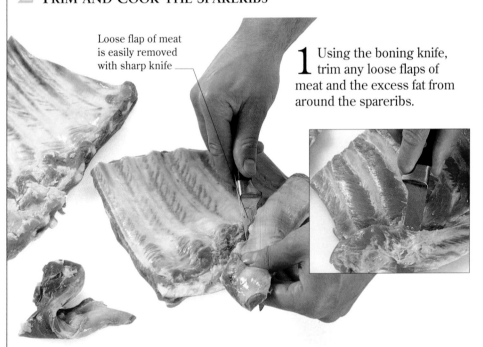

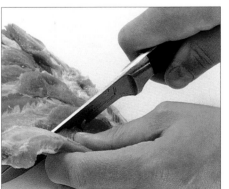

2 Cut down through the strips of meat between the bones to separate individual ribs.

ANNE SAYS
"If you are short of time, you could ask your butcher to prepare the spareribs for you."

HOW TO MAKE SCALLION BRUSHES

This is a simple decoration for spicy meats and salads.

1 Trim the roots and most of the green parts from the scallions, to form pieces that are about 2½-inches long.

2 Make slashes about ¾-inch deep at both ends of each piece. Spread the ends gently to open the slashes.

3 Put the scallions in a bowl of ice water and chill them until the fringed ends have curled, about 2 hours. Drain the scallions well before using.

3 Heat the oil in the wok, add the chili pepper, and cook until it turns dark brown, about 1 minute. Add 3–4 of the ribs and cook over high heat, stirring, until browned on all sides, 2–3 minutes.

4 Transfer the browned ribs to a plate using the tongs. Working in batches, brown the remaining ribs in the same way. Pour off all but about 2 tbsp oil from the wok.

5 Return all the browned ribs to the wok and pour in enough water so they are completely covered. Heat the liquid until it comes to a boil.

Pour in sufficient water to cover ribs

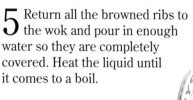

Chili pepper remains in wok and adds hot spice to spareribs

6 Reduce the heat and cover the wok. Simmer, stirring occasionally, about 1 hour. The ribs are cooked when the meat shrinks slightly on the bone, and feels tender when pierced with the tip of the small knife.

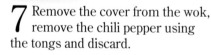

7 Remove the cover from the wok, remove the chili pepper using the tongs and discard.

8 Pour the sweet and sour sauce mixture into the cooked spareribs in the wok. Stir the mixture into the cooking liquid thoroughly to blend.

9 Simmer the mixture, stirring occasionally, until the liquid is reduced to a thick brown sauce, and the ribs are glazed, 25–30 minutes. If necessary, remove the ribs and reduce the sauce further by boiling fast.

Reduce sauce until thick enough to glaze ribs

Stir ribs occasionally to prevent sticking

¶◎¶ TO SERVE

Transfer the ribs to a warmed platter. Coat them with the sauce and decorate with scallion brushes.

Spareribs are glazed with tasty sauce

Scallion brushes add oriental touch

INDONESIAN SPICY SPARERIBS

Here spareribs are marinated in a spicy mixture, then simmered in the marinade, which reduces to a deep brown sauce.

1 Omit the sweet and sour sauce. Prepare the spareribs as directed.
2 Peel the skin from a 1-inch piece of fresh ginger root. Slice, cutting across the fibrous grain. Crush each slice of ginger with the flat of the knife, then finely chop. Peel and finely chop 4 garlic cloves.
3 In a small bowl, whisk together the chopped ginger, garlic, 6 tbsp dark soy sauce, 3 tbsp cider vinegar, 2 tbsp vegetable oil, 2 tbsp brown sugar, 1 tsp ground nutmeg, 1 tsp five-spice powder or ground allspice, ½ tsp ground cloves, and ½ tsp ground cinnamon.
4 Put the ribs in a shallow baking dish, pour the marinade over them, and turn the ribs so they are thoroughly coated. Cover the ribs and marinate in the refrigerator, turning occasionally, 2–3 hours.
5 Trim 2 scallions and cut them into thin diagonal slices using part of the green tops.
6 Remove the ribs from the marinade with a slotted spoon and pat dry with paper towels; reserve the marinade. Brown the ribs as directed, omitting the hot chili pepper. Pour off all but 2 tbsp oil from the wok, then add the marinade with the water to cover the ribs and simmer them until tender.
7 Boil to reduce the cooking liquid down to a thick sauce.
8 Transfer the ribs to warmed individual plates and spoon a little sauce over them. Sprinkle with the sliced scallions and serve, decorated with bouquets of fresh herbs.

MEXICAN TURNOVERS WITH CHICKEN AND CHEESE

Quesadillas con Pollo

🍽 SERVES 8 🥄 WORK TIME 35–40 MINUTES ♨ FRYING TIME 3–6 MINUTES*

EQUIPMENT

chef's knife

metal spatula

saucepan   small knife

wooden spoon

slotted spoon

rubber gloves   frying pan

bowls   cheese grater

chopping board

plastic wrap

ANNE SAYS
"*Instead of the frying pan, you can use a griddle for cooking the quesadillas. If it is large enough, cook 2–3 at a time.*"

These savory turnovers are a great way to use up cooked chicken. Mild Cheddar can be substituted for Monterey Jack.

**total frying time depends on size of frying pan*

SHOPPING LIST

2	medium onions
1 lb	tomatoes
	salt and pepper
3	fresh hot green chili peppers
4	garlic cloves
³/₄ lb	cooked boneless chicken
¹/₄ cup	vegetable oil, more if needed
¹/₂ cup	chicken stock or water
¹/₂ lb	Monterey Jack cheese
12	flour tortillas, each about 6 inches in diameter
	For the guacamole
5–7	sprigs of fresh coriander (cilantro)
1	small ripe tomato
1	small onion
1	garlic clove
1	ripe avocado
2–3	drops of Tabasco sauce
	juice of ¹/₂ lime

INGREDIENTS

cooked chicken

flour tortillas †

chicken stock

hot chili peppers   onions

lime juice

avocado

tomatoes   vegetable oil   Monterey Jack cheese

garlic cloves

Tabasco sauce

fresh coriander

†corn tortillas can also be used

ORDER OF WORK

1 **MAKE THE QUESADILLA GARNISH AND FILLING**

2 **MAKE THE GUACAMOLE**

3 **COOK THE QUESADILLAS**

1 MAKE THE QUESADILLA GARNISH AND FILLING

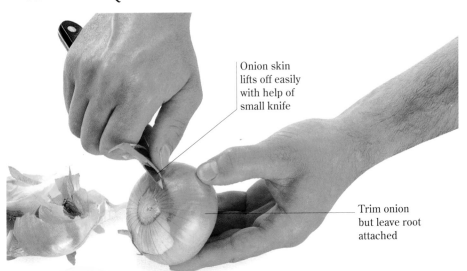

Onion skin lifts off easily with help of small knife

Trim onion but leave root attached

1 Peel the onions, leaving a little of the root attached. Cut lengthwise in half. Lay each onion half flat on the chopping board and slice horizontally toward the root, leaving the slices attached at the root end, then slice vertically, again leaving the root end uncut. Cut across each onion half to make dice.

2 Peel, seed, and chop the tomatoes (see box, page 104). Combine the tomatoes with one-quarter of the chopped onion. Season to taste with salt and pepper; set aside for garnish.

4 Cut the cored chili peppers into thin rings and reserve for garnish. Core, seed, and dice the remaining chili pepper (see box, page 106).

Rubber gloves prevent chili peppers burning your skin

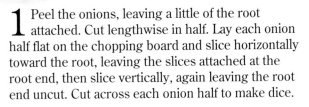

3 Slice off the stems from 2 of the chili peppers; remove the cores and seeds with a teaspoon or by tapping the peppers against the work surface.

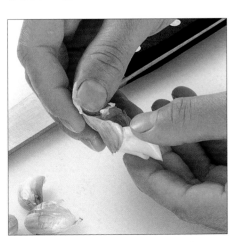

5 Set the flat side of the chef's knife on top of each garlic clove and strike it with your fist. Discard the skin; finely chop the garlic.

6 Pull the chicken meat into shreds with your fingers, discarding any skin and sinews.

HOW TO PEEL, SEED, AND CHOP TOMATOES

Tomatoes are often peeled and seeded before they are chopped, so they can be cooked to a smooth purée, eliminating the necessity to strain the mixture.

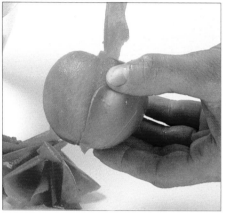

1 Bring a small pan of water to a boil. Cut the cores from the tomatoes. Score an "x" on the base of each tomato. Immerse the tomatoes in the water until the skin starts to split. Transfer them at once to a bowl of cold water to stop cooking.

2 Peel the skin from the tomatoes with the help of a small knife. Cut the tomatoes crosswise in half and squeeze out the seeds.

3 Set each tomato half cut-side down and slice it. Give it a half turn and slice again. Chop the flesh coarsely or finely, as required.

7 Heat 3 tbsp oil in the frying pan. Add the remaining chopped onion, the garlic, and the diced chili pepper, and cook until the onions are soft but not brown, 2–3 minutes.

8 Add the chicken stock and simmer until almost all the liquid has evaporated, 5–7 minutes. Stir in the chicken and cook 1–2 minutes. Season to taste. Transfer the mixture to a bowl and wipe the frying pan. Grate the cheese.

Shredded chicken takes on flavor from reduced stock

2 MAKE THE GUACAMOLE

1 Strip the coriander leaves from the stems and pile the leaves on the chopping board. With the chef's knife, finely chop the leaves. Peel, seed, and finely chop the tomato (see box, page 104).

2 Peel and chop the onion and garlic. Place the chopped tomato, coriander, onion, and garlic in a bowl and toss to combine.

3 Cut lengthwise around the avocado, through to the pit. Twist to loosen the halves and pull them apart. With a chopping movement, embed the blade of the chef's knife in the pit and lift it free. Scrape the avocado pulp into the bowl.

ANNE SAYS
"You can scoop out the pit with a spoon."

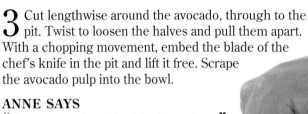

Teaspoon scoops all avocado pulp from skin

4 Combine the guacamole ingredients with a fork, mashing the avocado against the side of the bowl. Add a pinch of salt and a few drops of Tabasco.

Ripe avocado pulp will blend easily

5 Add the lime juice and stir well to mix. Taste for seasoning. Cover and refrigerate until serving.

3 COOK THE QUESADILLAS

1 Heat the oven to low for keeping the quesadillas warm. Heat the remaining oil in the frying pan and add 1 tortilla. Sprinkle with about 2 tbsp grated cheese, leaving a ½-inch border. Put about 2 spoonfuls chicken mixture on top of the cheese and cook until the cheese begins to melt.

Spoon chicken over cheese in even layer leaving border

HOW TO CORE, SEED, AND DICE FRESH HOT CHILI PEPPERS

Fresh hot chili peppers must be finely chopped so their flavor is spread evenly through the dish. For a hotter flavor you can add the seeds, too. Chili peppers can burn your skin, so be sure to wear rubber gloves and to avoid contact with eyes.

1 Cut the chili peppers lengthwise in half with a small knife.

2 Cut out the core and fleshy white ribs and scrape out the seeds.

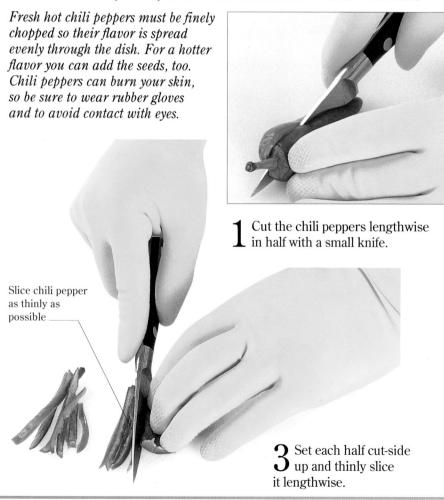

Slice chili pepper as thinly as possible

3 Set each half cut-side up and thinly slice it lengthwise.

4 Hold the strips together and cut across into very fine dice.

2 Using the metal spatula, fold the quesadilla over in half to enclose the filling. Cook the quesadilla until the tortilla is crispy and golden brown, 1–2 minutes.

3 Turn the quesadilla over and cook until crispy. Transfer to a heatproof plate and keep warm in the oven while cooking the remaining quesadillas, adding oil to the pan if necessary.

🍴 **TO SERVE**

Halve the quesadillas and serve 3 halves on each plate with the guacamole, tomato-onion garnish, and chili pepper rings. Decorate with coriander, if you like.

Crisp tortillas
enclose delicious
Mexican filling

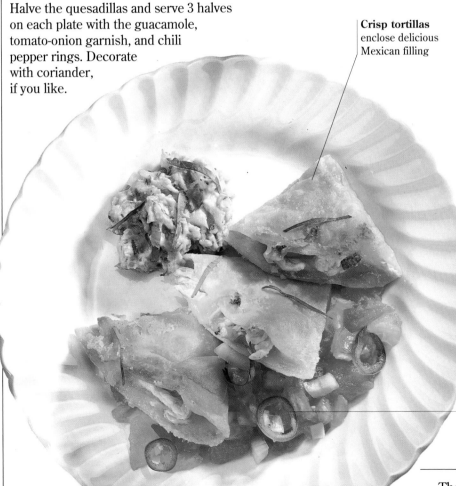

Chili pepper rings
add decorative touch

VARIATION

MEXICAN TURNOVERS WITH PORK

Cubes of pork add body to the filling for these quesadillas.

1 Prepare the filling ingredients, but omit the chicken and instead cut 1 lb cooked boneless pork into 1-inch cubes. Use only 2 hot chili peppers and dice both of them. Use 2 oz Cheddar cheese instead of the Monterey Jack. Chop the leaves from 5–7 sprigs of fresh coriander (cilantro).
2 Sauté all of the chopped onion with the garlic and diced chili peppers, then add the pork and cook until browned, 3–5 minutes longer. Omit the chicken stock or water and stir in the chopped tomatoes. Continue cooking until the filling is slightly thick, 5–7 minutes. Taste for seasoning; let cool slightly.
3 Omit the guacamole. Cook the quesadillas as directed, sprinkling each one with 1–2 tsp of Cheddar cheese and a pinch of chopped coriander before adding the filling and folding over the quesadillas.
4 Cut the quesadillas into halves and serve decorated with red onion rings and coriander sprigs, if you like.

— **GETTING AHEAD** —
The chicken filling can be made up to 1 day ahead and kept, covered, in the refrigerator. The guacamole can be made up to 1 day ahead and refrigerated, tightly covered.

PROSCIUTTO PIZZAS WITH MOZZARELLA AND BASIL

🍴 MAKES 8　🥣 WORK TIME 50–55 MINUTES*　🍲 BAKING TIME 10–12 MINUTES

EQUIPMENT

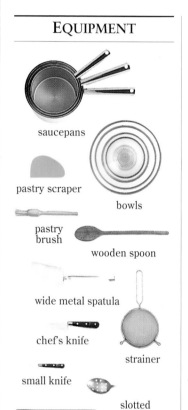

saucepans

pastry scraper

bowls

pastry brush

wooden spoon

wide metal spatula

chef's knife

strainer

small knife

slotted spoon

plastic wrap

chopping board

2 baking sheets†

rolling pin

†pizza stone can be used instead of 1 baking sheet

ANNE SAYS
"*When mixing and kneading the pizza dough you can use an electric mixer fitted with a dough hook instead of your hands.*"

Individual pizzas are a welcome opening to any meal. Prosciutto, tomato sauce, melted mozzarella, and fresh basil form the topping for these.

GETTING AHEAD
The pizza dough and tomato sauce can be made up to 12 hours ahead and kept refrigerated. Assemble the pizzas and bake them just before serving.

*plus about 1 hour or overnight rising time

INGREDIENTS

prosciutto†

fresh basil

mozzarella cheese

olive oil

flour

active dry yeast

tomatoes‡

onion

sugar

garlic clove

tomato paste

†country ham can also be used

‡plum tomatoes can also be used

SHOPPING LIST

For the pizza dough	
1½ tsp	active dry yeast or ½ cake (9 g) compressed yeast
1 cup	lukewarm water
2½ cups	flour, more if needed
2 tbsp	olive oil, more for bowl
	salt and pepper
For the topping	
1¼ lb	tomatoes
1	small onion
1	garlic clove
1-2 tbsp	olive oil
1½ tbsp	tomato paste
1	pinch of sugar
3 oz	thinly sliced prosciutto
12 oz	mozzarella cheese
1	small bunch of fresh basil

ORDER OF WORK

1 MAKE AND KNEAD THE PIZZA DOUGH

2 PREPARE THE TOPPING

3 ASSEMBLE AND BAKE THE PIZZAS

1 MAKE AND KNEAD THE PIZZA DOUGH

1 Sprinkle or crumble the yeast over 2–3 tbsp of the water in a small bowl; let stand until dissolved, 5 minutes. Sift the flour, 1 tsp salt, and ½ tsp pepper. Make a well in the center; add the dissolved yeast mixture, the remaining water, and the oil. Work the ingredients together.

2 Draw in the flour with the pastry scraper and work it into the other ingredients with your fingertips to form a smooth dough.

3 Peel back the dough in one piece, then shape it into a loose ball, and turn it 90 degrees. Continue kneading the dough by pushing it away from you and gathering it up into a ball, until it is smooth and very elastic, 5–8 minutes.

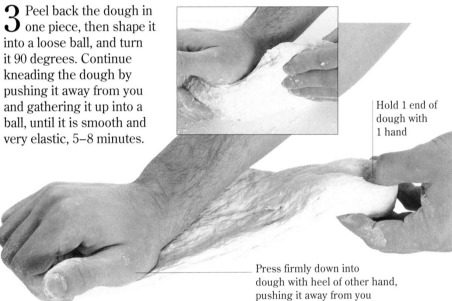

Hold 1 end of dough with 1 hand

Press firmly down into dough with heel of other hand, pushing it away from you

4 Lightly oil a large bowl. Transfer the dough to the bowl, cover with plastic wrap, and let rise in a warm place until doubled in bulk, about 1 hour. Alternatively, leave the dough to rise overnight in the refrigerator.

2 PREPARE THE TOPPING

1 Cut the cores from the tomatoes; score an "x" on the base of each. Immerse in boiling water until the skin starts to split. Transfer to cold water. When cooled, peel and cut crosswise in half; squeeze out the seeds, then chop each half.

Coarsely chop each tomato half

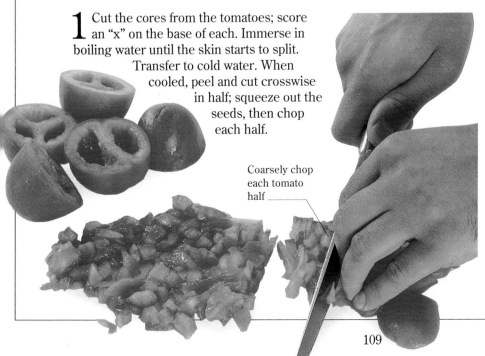

2 Peel the onion, leaving a little of the root attached, and cut it lengthwise in half. Lay each onion half flat on the chopping board and slice horizontally, then vertically. Finally, cut across the onion to make dice.

3 Set the flat side of the chef's knife on top of the garlic clove and strike it with your fist. Discard the skin and finely chop the garlic.

Add tomatoes to softened onion and garlic

4 Heat the olive oil in a small saucepan and sauté the onion and garlic until soft but not brown, 1–2 minutes. Stir in the tomatoes, tomato paste, salt, pepper, and a pinch of sugar. Cook, stirring occasionally, until the sauce is thick, 7–10 minutes.

5 With the chef's knife, cut the prosciutto slices across into fairly narrow strips.

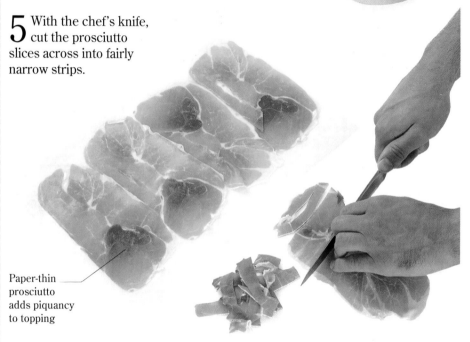

Paper-thin prosciutto adds piquancy to topping

6 Thinly slice the mozzarella cheese. Strip the basil leaves from the stems; reserve some sprigs for garnish.

3 **ASSEMBLE AND BAKE THE PIZZAS**

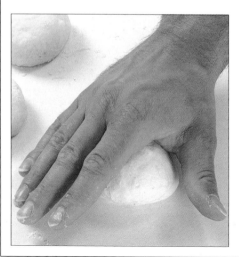

1 Heat the oven to 450° F. Heat one baking sheet or a pizza stone near the bottom of the oven. Generously sprinkle the other baking sheet with flour. Knead the pizza dough lightly to knock out the air and cut it into 8 equal pieces. Lightly flour the work surface. Shape 4 pieces of dough into balls.

2 Roll each ball into a round with the rolling pin, then roll and pull each one into a 6-inch round. Transfer to the floured baking sheet.

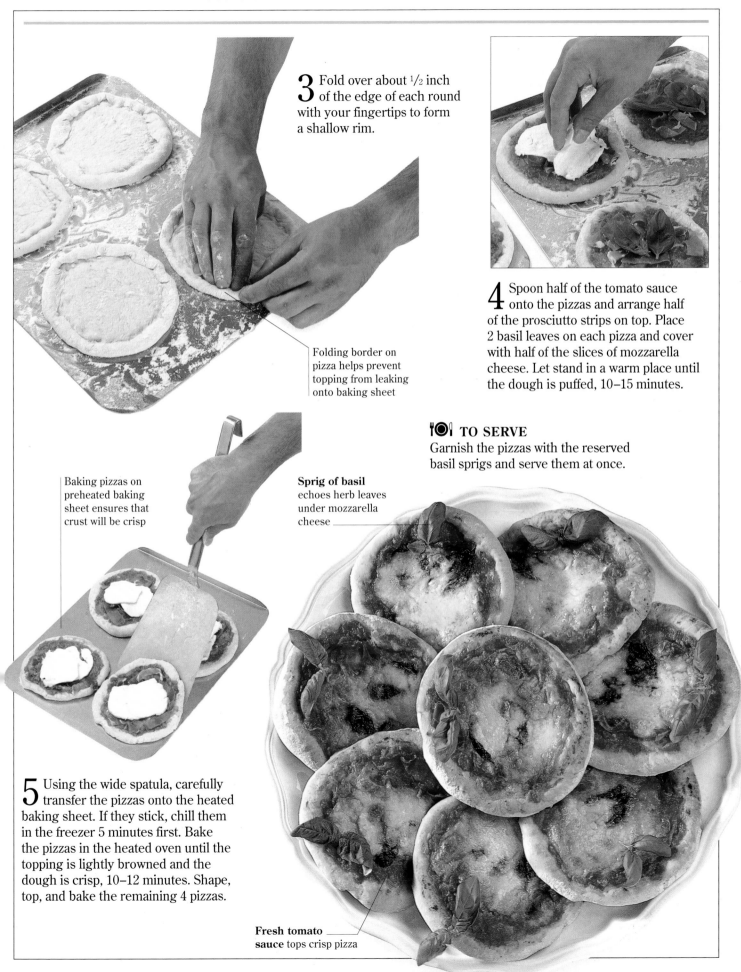

3 Fold over about ½ inch of the edge of each round with your fingertips to form a shallow rim.

Folding border on pizza helps prevent topping from leaking onto baking sheet

4 Spoon half of the tomato sauce onto the pizzas and arrange half of the prosciutto strips on top. Place 2 basil leaves on each pizza and cover with half of the slices of mozzarella cheese. Let stand in a warm place until the dough is puffed, 10–15 minutes.

🍴 **TO SERVE**
Garnish the pizzas with the reserved basil sprigs and serve them at once.

Baking pizzas on preheated baking sheet ensures that crust will be crisp

Sprig of basil echoes herb leaves under mozzarella cheese

5 Using the wide spatula, carefully transfer the pizzas onto the heated baking sheet. If they stick, chill them in the freezer 5 minutes first. Bake the pizzas in the heated oven until the topping is lightly browned and the dough is crisp, 10–12 minutes. Shape, top, and bake the remaining 4 pizzas.

Fresh tomato sauce tops crisp pizza

TROPICAL SHRIMP KEBABS

 SERVES 8 WORK TIME 20–25 MINUTES* 🍲 BROILING TIME 4–6 MINUTES

EQUIPMENT

saucepans, 1 with lid

shallow non-metallic dish

strainer

pastry brush

small knife

bowls

chef's knife

cheesecloth

whisk

wooden spoon

8 bamboo skewers†

chopping board

† bamboo skewers need to be soaked in water 30 minutes before use; metal skewers can also be used – they do not need to be soaked

INGREDIENTS

fresh coriander

shrimp

fresh ginger root

soy sauce

garlic cloves

lime juice

vegetable oil

crunchy peanut butter

brown sugar

onion

chili powder

dried hot red pepper flakes

unsweetened shredded coconut

Marinated shrimp, served with a peanut sauce, make a great opener for a summer meal. They can be broiled indoors or grilled on a barbecue.

plus 1–2 hours marinating time

SHOPPING LIST

½-inch	piece of fresh ginger root
2	large garlic cloves
1	small bunch of fresh coriander (cilantro)
½ cup	vegetable oil, more for broiler rack
6 tbsp	lime juice, from 2 limes
½ tsp	sugar, more to taste
½ tsp	chili powder
1 tbsp	soy sauce
32	large raw shrimp, total weight about 1½ lb
	salt and pepper
	For the peanut sauce
1 cup	unsweetened shredded coconut
1	small onion
2	large garlic cloves
¼ cup	vegetable oil
½ tsp	dried hot red pepper flakes
	juice of ½ lime
2 tsp	soy sauce
⅓ cup	crunchy peanut butter
1 tsp	brown sugar

ORDER OF WORK

1. **MARINATE THE SHRIMP**

2. **MAKE THE PEANUT SAUCE**

3. **BROIL THE SHRIMP**

112

1 MARINATE THE SHRIMP

Chopped leaves
release flavor

1 Peel and chop the ginger (see box, page 116). Set the flat side of the chef's knife on top of each garlic clove and strike it with your fist. Discard the skin and finely chop the garlic.

2 Strip the coriander leaves from the stems and pile them on the chopping board. With the chef's knife, coarsely chop the leaves.

3 Whisk together the oil, lime juice, ginger, and chopped garlic. Add the sugar, chili powder, chopped coriander, soy sauce, and salt to taste; stir well to mix.

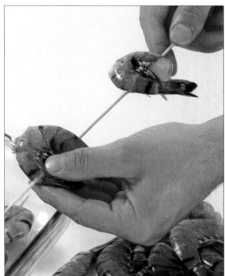

Distribute marinade evenly over shrimp

The longer shrimp are left to marinate, the more piquant their flavor

4 Thread 4 shrimp on each bamboo skewer, laying each completed skewer in the shallow dish.

ANNE SAYS
"If using metal skewers, marinate the shrimp, then put them on the skewers."

5 Pour the marinade over the shrimp. Cover and let marinate in the refrigerator 1–2 hours, turning the skewers occasionally. Meanwhile, make the peanut sauce (see page 114).

2 MAKE THE PEANUT SAUCE

Shredded coconut is infused in boiling water

1 Bring 1 cup water to a boil in a small saucepan. Add the coconut and stir. Cover, and set aside 30 minutes. Meanwhile, finely chop the onion (see box, page 115) and the garlic.

2 Heat the oil in another small saucepan. Add the onion and cook, stirring, until lightly browned, 2–3 minutes. Add the garlic and the hot red pepper flakes and continue cooking until the onion is golden.

! TAKE CARE !
Do not let the garlic brown or it will be bitter.

3 Add the lime juice and soy sauce to the onion mixture; stir to combine. Remove from the heat.

Line strainer with large piece of cheesecloth

4 Stir in the peanut butter and brown sugar. Let cool.

5 Put a piece of cheesecloth in the strainer, set over a bowl. Pour in the coconut and its liquid.

HOW TO CHOP AN ONION

The size of dice depends on the thickness of the initial slices. For a standard size, make slices that are about ¼-inch thick. For finely chopped onions, slice as thinly as possible.

1 Peel the onion and trim the top; leave a little of the root attached to hold the onion together.

2 Cut the onion lengthwise in half, through root and stem. Place each half cut-side down.

3 Hold the onion half steady with one hand. Make a series of horizontal cuts from the top toward the root but not through it.

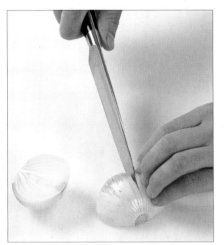

4 Make a series of lengthwise vertical cuts, cutting just to the root but not through it.

ANNE SAYS
"When slicing, tuck your fingertips under and use your knuckles to guide the blade of the knife."

5 Slice the onion crosswise into dice. For finely chopped onion, continue chopping until you have the fineness required.

Knuckles guide chef's knife when slicing onion

6 Gather up the ends of the cloth and squeeze the coconut well to extract as much liquid or "milk" as possible. Discard the coconut.

Unsweetened shredded, coconut yields deliciously perfumed milk when steeped in boiling water

7 Pour the coconut milk into the peanut sauce, and stir until the sauce is evenly mixed. Season to taste with salt and pepper and let stand.

ANNE SAYS
"The peanut sauce may separate on standing. Heat it gently and stir in 1–2 tbsp water to re-emulsify it."

3 BROIL THE SHRIMP

Brushing with marinade
keeps shrimp moist
during broiling

1 Heat the broiler. Brush the broiler rack with oil. Transfer the kebabs from the dish to the rack, reserving the marinade for brushing.

2 Brush the kebabs with marinade. Broil the kebabs 2–3 inches from the heat until the shrimp are pink, brushing with marinade occasionally, 2–3 minutes.

Kebabs are broiled on
rack so excess marinade
drips onto pan

HOW TO PEEL AND CHOP FRESH GINGER

It is important to chop ginger root quite finely, so the flavor is released and spreads evenly throughout the dish.

Gather ginger
slices together
with your fingers
as you chop

1 With a small knife, peel the skin from the ginger root. Using a chef's knife, slice the ginger, cutting across the fibrous grain.

2 Place the chef's knife flat on each slice of ginger root and crush with your hand.

3 Chop the slices of ginger root until they become quite fine.

3 Turn the kebabs and brush again with marinade. Continue broiling until the shrimp are pink on the other side, 2–3 minutes longer.

🍽 TO SERVE

Set a kebab on each of 8 plates and accompany with a small bowl of peanut sauce. A few salad leaves, chopped herbs, tomato wedges, and lemon triangles make a colorful decoration.

V A R I A T I O N
VIETNAMESE SHRIMP KEBABS

In this alternative to broiled shrimp kebabs, the shrimp are puréed, then coated with coconut and baked.

1 Omit the marinade. Make the peanut sauce as directed, using 3 chopped garlic cloves.
2 Peel the shrimp, reserving 8 in their shells.
3 Make a shallow cut along the back of each peeled shrimp and remove the dark intestinal vein.
4 Put the peeled shrimp in a food processor with 1 egg, 1 peeled garlic clove, 1½ tbsp soy sauce, 1½ tbsp Asian fish sauce or 1 tsp anchovy paste, 2 tsp vegetable oil, 1 tbsp flour, ½ tsp sugar, salt, and pepper. Work to a smooth purée. Transfer to a bowl, cover and chill until firm, 1–1½ hours.
5 Heat the oven to 400° F. Oil 8 metal skewers. Combine ½ cup unsweetened shredded coconut with 2 tbsp dried breadcrumbs on a baking sheet. Wet the palms of your hands and roll the shrimp mixture into 1-inch balls. Using 2 forks, toss each one in the coconut mixture until coated.
6 Thread the shrimp balls onto the oiled skewers, with 1 reserved unpeeled shrimp on each, and lay them on an oiled baking sheet. Bake in the heated oven until the shrimp balls are firm to the touch and the whole shrimp are pink, 6–8 minutes. Serve at once with the peanut sauce.
7 Introduce splashes of color to each serving with carrot julienne, lemon twists, and a dill sprig, if you like.

Shrimp are served in their shells, leaving guests to peel them at the table

GETTING AHEAD
The shrimp can be marinated up to 4 hours ahead in the refrigerator. Cook them just before serving.

CHEDDAR CHEESE AND ZUCCHINI SOUFFLE

🍽 SERVES 6   🥣 WORK TIME 30–35 MINUTES   🍲 BAKING TIME 25–30 MINUTES

EQUIPMENT

2-quart soufflé dish

pastry brush

chef's knife

bowls

whisk

grater

wooden spoon

saucepans

strainer

frying pan

chopping board

metal bowl

rubber spatula

Grated zucchini and Cheddar cheese give a pleasing green- and orange-speckled appearance to this classic savory soufflé. Use sharp or mild Cheddar according to your taste. A straight-sided soufflé dish is the key to a successful soufflé.

GETTING AHEAD

The zucchini mixture for the soufflé can be prepared up to 3 hours ahead. Whisk the egg whites and finish the soufflé just before baking.

SHOPPING LIST

1 lb	zucchini
2	shallots
2 tbsp	unsalted butter, more for soufflé dish
	salt and pepper
4	eggs
3 oz	Cheddar cheese
2	egg whites
	For the white cream sauce
3/4 cup	milk
2 tbsp	unsalted butter
3 tbsp	flour
1/2 cup	heavy cream
	ground nutmeg

INGREDIENTS

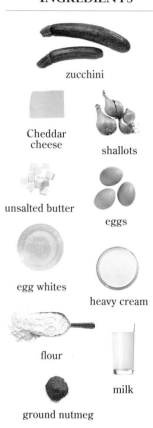

zucchini

Cheddar cheese

shallots

unsalted butter

eggs

egg whites

heavy cream

flour

milk

ground nutmeg

ORDER OF WORK

1 **PREPARE THE ZUCCHINI**

2 **MAKE THE WHITE CREAM SAUCE**

3 **MAKE THE SOUFFLE BASE**

4 **FINISH AND BAKE THE SOUFFLE**

1 PREPARE THE ZUCCHINI

1 Trim the zucchini and grate them coarsely onto a plate.

Zucchini skin adds color to soufflé

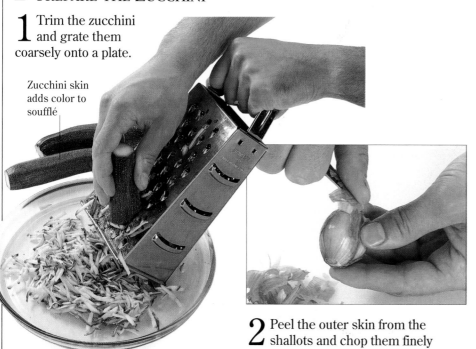

2 Peel the outer skin from the shallots and chop them finely (see box, right).

3 Melt the butter in the frying pan. Stir in the shallots and cook over medium heat, until soft, about 2 minutes. Add the zucchini, salt, and pepper and cook, stirring, until the zucchini is just tender, 3–5 minutes.

Do not overcook zucchini or crunchy texture will be lost

4 Transfer the sautéed zucchini to the strainer set over a medium bowl and allow the liquid from the zucchini to drain thoroughly.

HOW TO CHOP A SHALLOT

For a standard chop, make slices that are about $1/8$-inch thick. For a fine chop, slice the shallot as thinly as possible.

1 Peel the outer, papery skin from the shallot. If necessary, separate the shallot into sections at the root and peel the sections. Set each one flat-side down on a chopping board. Hold the shallot steady with your fingers and slice horizontally, leaving the slices attached at the root end.

2 Slice vertically through the shallot, again leaving the root end uncut.

3 Cut across the shallot to make fine dice. Continue chopping, if necessary, until it is very fine.

2 MAKE THE WHITE CREAM SAUCE

1 Scald the milk in a small saucepan. Melt the butter in a medium saucepan. Over the heat, add the flour all at once and cook, whisking briskly, until the mixture starts to foam, 30–60 seconds.

Whisk flour vigorously into melted butter

Do not let butter and flour brown

To avoid lumps, whisk constantly when adding milk

2 Remove the pan from the heat and let the mixture cool slightly. Then slowly pour in the hot milk, whisking all the time, and continue to whisk until well mixed.

3 Return to the heat and cook the sauce, whisking constantly.

! TAKE CARE !
If the sauce forms lumps at any stage, stop heating and whisk vigorously. If whisking is not sufficient to remove lumps, strain the sauce.

4 When the sauce boils and thickens, pour in the cream and whisk until thoroughly combined. Season to taste with salt, pepper, and a pinch of nutmeg. Simmer 2 minutes longer. Remove from the heat and set aside.

3 MAKE THE SOUFFLE BASE

1 Separate the eggs. Coarsely grate the Cheddar cheese.

Coarsely grated cheese will melt into hot sauce ⎯

2 If necessary, reheat the white cream sauce just to a boil. Remove from the heat, whisk the egg yolks into the hot sauce, one at a time, whisking well after each addition.

3 Return the pan to the heat. Bring the mixture back to a boil, whisking constantly, and simmer 1 minute longer to ensure that the egg yolks are fully cooked.

Sautéed zucchini will blend easily into cheese mixture

Stir grated cheese into sauce off heat so cheese melts but does not form strings

4 Remove the pan from the heat and stir the grated Cheddar cheese into the warm mixture.

5 Stir the drained zucchini into the sauce. Taste for seasoning and adjust if necessary; the soufflé base should be highly seasoned.

4 FINISH AND BAKE THE SOUFFLE

1 Heat the oven to 375° F. Melt a little butter and grease the side and base of the soufflé dish using the pastry brush. Reheat the zucchini mixture until hot to the touch.

2 Beat the 6 egg whites with a pinch of salt in the metal bowl, using the whisk or an electric mixer until stiff peaks form, 3–5 minutes.

! TAKE CARE !
Do not overbeat the egg whites or they will become grainy.

3 Add about one-quarter of the beaten egg whites to the warm zucchini and cheese mixture and gently stir with the rubber spatula until well mixed.

Lightened zucchini mixture folds easily into egg whites

Rolling motion ensures mixtures are combined, with minimum loss of volume

4 Add the lightened zucchini and egg white mixture to the remaining egg whites in the bowl. Fold the mixture together: cut down into the center of the bowl with the spatula, scoop under the contents, and turn them over in a rolling motion. At the same time, with your other hand, turn the bowl counter-clockwise. Continue folding until the egg whites are thoroughly incorporated.

Egg whites and soufflé base are thoroughly blended together

Use rubber spatula to scrape all soufflé mixture from bowl

5 Pour the soufflé mixture into the prepared dish. Bake in the heated oven until puffed and brown, 25–30 minutes.

ANNE SAYS
"Do not overcook the soufflé – the center should be quite soft."

🍴 TO SERVE
Serve immediately: plunge 2 large metal spoons into the center of the soufflé and scoop out a wedge for each serving – it will lose volume within minutes as it cools.

Flecks of green zucchini are striking contrast to golden Cheddar cheese

Soufflé is crusty brown on outside and moist in center

ONION AND SAGE SOUFFLE

The classic combination of onion and sage is the basis for this soufflé.

1 Omit the zucchini, shallots, and Cheddar cheese.
2 Peel 8 medium onions (about 2 lb total weight), leaving a little of the root attached, and cut them in half through root and stem, using a chef's knife. Lay each onion half flat on a chopping board and cut across into thin slices.
3 Melt 3 tbsp butter in a medium saucepan. Add the onions with salt and pepper, press a piece of buttered foil on top, and cover with the lid. Cook very gently, stirring occasionally, until the onions are very soft but not brown, 15–20 minutes. Remove the lid and foil and cook, stirring, until any liquid has evaporated.
4 Meanwhile, strip the leaves from 5–7 sprigs of fresh sage and pile them on the chopping board. With the chef's knife, finely chop the leaves.
5 Make the white cream sauce as directed.
6 Add the onions and sage to the sauce. Finish and bake the soufflé as directed.

APPETIZERS KNOW-HOW

An appetizer's role in a meal is to whet the imagination as well as the appetite. Full-flavored ingredients help to achieve this end, in teasingly small portions. No hard and fast rules dictate what the first course of any meal should contain. There are, however, some practical guidelines that will help you select an appropriate appetizer, taking into account the occasion, the type of meal you are serving, the time of year, and the number of people.

CHOOSING APPETIZERS

The appetizer sets the scene for the whole meal, so first consider the dishes that are to follow. If you are serving a hearty main course, you might want to opt for a light and simple appetizer, such as Marinated Goat Cheese Salad or Italian Toasts with Olives, Tomatoes, and Anchovies. Likewise, if the main course is lighter, a more substantial appetizer like Prosciutto Pizzas with Mozzarella and Basil might be more welcome.

If the meal you are serving has more than three courses, you should consider reducing the appetizer quantity so your guests do not spoil their appetites. Elegantly diminutive portions can easily be made from recipes such as Herbed Salmon Cakes or Stuffed Mushrooms with Herbs, and a dish like Chicken Liver and Apple Pâté can be served in delicate little egg cups for smaller portions.

Consider also the ambience of the meal you will be serving. For your family and friends, Clams Steamed in White Wine is convivial, served steaming in a large bowl right on the table with plenty of crusty bread for sopping up the juices. Offer the Szechuan Sweet and Sour Spareribs at a casual meal where everyone can leave their knives and forks and use their fingers. If the meal is a more formal affair, you may look toward Poached Scallops in Cider Sauce served in their shells, or Oysters in Champagne Sauce, or Smoked Trout Mousse with Horseradish and Dill.

Menus may have a theme, carried out from starter to dessert. For example, Spring Rolls with Lettuce and Mint Leaves might be the opening for an Asian dinner, or Steamed Mussels with Saffron-Cream Sauce might create a French bistro mood. Don't hesitate to break away from tradition by mixing and matching themes and cuisines that are compatible. Always keep in mind, however, that a pungent or spicy appetizer should lead into an equally forceful main course, because pepper and spice will dull the palate for more delicate foods to come.

APPETIZERS AND YOUR HEALTH

If you are concerned about calories and fat content, here are some points to consider when preparing appetizers. First of all look for recipes that rely on ingredients naturally low in fat, such as Chinese-Style Stuffed Tomatoes or Greek-Style Piquant Vegetables. Then turn to dishes containing added fat that can be eliminated; for instance, omit the peanut sauce from Tropical Shrimp Kebabs and serve them plain or with a vinaigrette dressing. Substitute yogurt for the sour cream that accompanies Blini with Smoked Salmon, and reduce the amount of oil that moistens Italian Toasts with Olives, Tomatoes, and Anchovies. In recipes that require pan-frying or sautéing, a non-stick pan will allow you to reduce the cooking fat to a minimum. Replace butter with a polyunsaturated oil, such as safflower oil. In pastry recipes, a polyunsaturated margarine can replace the butter, although the flavor will be less rich.

PREPARING APPETIZERS AHEAD

The art of entertaining relies on organization, preparing as much as possible in advance so that you can spend more time with your guests. Even for family dinners at home, you will want to be at the table and not at the stove.

For dinner parties, dishes such as Raw Beef Salad with Capers and Chicken Liver and Apple Pâté can be fully prepared, arranged on individual plates, and covered a few hours in advance. Other dishes, such as Stuffed Grape Leaves, Greek-Style Piquant Vegetables, and Smoked Trout Mousse with Horseradish and Dill, can be completed at least a day in advance and left covered in the refrigerator, to be transferred to serving bowls, or unmolded onto plates just before serving. All of these appetizers are as appropriate for a buffet as for a seated meal.

Other recipes may require quick reheating before being brought to the table, but they too can be made a day ahead: Sautéed Onion and Roquefort Tart, Szechuan Sweet and Sour Spareribs, and Stuffed Mushrooms with Herbs are in this category, to name a few. No recipes have to be prepared totally at the last minute. At the very least, certain parts of cooking and assembly can be done in advance, such as chopping vegetables or making pastry shells, freeing you to take care of other things before the meal is served. So before you embark on an appetizer, read the section on Getting Ahead carefully to be sure that the preparation plan it describes fits into your schedule.

MICROWAVE COOKING

Many of these recipes can be adapted for microwave cooking, speeding up their preparation. For Stuffed Grape Leaves, for example, you can toast the pine nuts, prepare the rice stuffing, and cook the stuffed leaves in the microwave. Cooking time for Stuffed Mushrooms with Herbs is greatly reduced by using the microwave. Greek-Style Piquant Vegetables can be microwaved, and Clams Steamed in White Wine can be steamed open in the microwave.

In other recipes, you can prepare ingredients quickly by using the microwave oven. The salmon fillet for Herbed Salmon Cakes can be poached in the microwave, although the cakes themselves are best cooked on top of the stove for a golden, crispy exterior. In Sautéed Onion and Roquefort Tart, the onions cook quickly in the microwave, and you can rapidly wilt the cabbage for Cabbage and Goat Cheese Tart.

Don't forget that some basic techniques are easy in the microwave. You can peel the skin from onions, garlic, and tomatoes: heat onions and garlic cloves at High (100% power); put tomatoes in boiling water in a microwave-safe bowl and cook until the skin splits. You can also cook bacon and even prove yeast dough in the microwave.

HOW-TO BOXES

Some basic techniques appear in a number of recipes and they are shown in extra detail in these special "how-to" boxes:

CHICKEN STOCK

🍽 MAKES ABOUT 2 QUARTS

🥣 WORK TIME 15 MINUTES

🍲 COOKING TIME UP TO 3 HOURS

SHOPPING LIST

2– 2¹⁄₂ lb	chicken backs and necks
1	onion, quartered
1	carrot, quartered
1	celery stalk, quartered
1	bouquet garni
5	peppercorns
2 quarts	water, more if needed to cover

1 Put the chicken pieces in a large pot with the remaining ingredients.

2 Bring to a boil. Simmer up to 3 hours, skimming occasionally with a large metal spoon.

3 Strain the stock into a large bowl. Cool, then cover, and keep in the refrigerator.

FISH STOCK

🍽 MAKES ABOUT 1 QUART

🥣 WORK TIME 10–15 MINUTES

🍲 COOKING TIME 20 MINUTES

SHOPPING LIST

1 lb	fish bones and heads, cut into 2-inch pieces
1	onion, thinly sliced
1 cup	dry white wine
1 quart	water
3–5	sprigs of parsley
1 tsp	peppercorns

1 Wash the fish bones and heads; place them in a medium saucepan with the remaining ingredients.

2 Bring to a boil and simmer 20 minutes, skimming occasionally with a large metal spoon.

3 Strain the stock into a bowl. Cool, then cover, and keep in the refrigerator.

INDEX

ACKNOWLEDGMENTS

Photographers David Murray
Jules Selmes
Photographer's Assistant Ian Boddy

Chef Eric Treuille
Cookery Consultant Annie Nichols
Assisted by Jane Stevenson

US Editor Jeanette Mall

Typesetting Linda Parker
Text film by Disc to Print (UK) Limited

Production Consultant Lorraine Baird

*Anne Willan would like to thank her
chief editor Kate Krader, associate editors
Stacy Toporoff and Jacqueline Bobrow,
and consultant editor Cynthia Nims, for
their vital help with writing this book
and researching and testing the recipes,
aided by La Varenne's chefs and trainees.*